MARRYING AN IGBO MAN:

A GUIDE TO UNDERSTANDING CULTURE, LOVE, AND FAMILY

Understanding Igbo Culture And Marriage: Insights For Non-Igbo Women On Cross-Cultural Marriages With Igbo Men

Dr. Godwin Ude, MBA, PhD

Table Of Contents

Figure 1: An Igbo Man with his Caucasian Bride during a Western-themed wedding ceremony

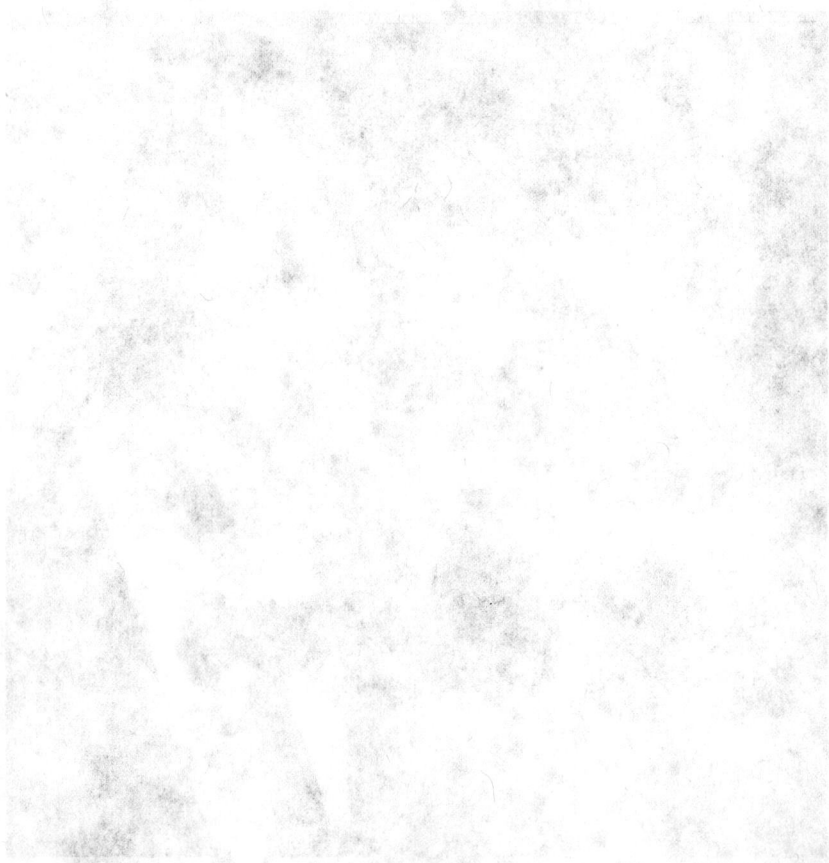

INTRODUCTION

Cross-cultural marriages offer a unique blend of challenges and rewards, often bridging diverse cultural traditions and shared human experiences. *"Marrying an Igbo Man: A Guide to Understanding Culture, Love, and Family"* by Dr. Godwin Ude delves into the intricacies of such unions, offering a comprehensive guide for non-Igbo women and others interested in understanding Igbo culture, relationships, and family dynamics. With its dual structure of research-backed insights and real-life narratives, this book emerges as a vital resource for building harmonious and enduring cross-cultural marriages.

The Purpose of the Book

At its core, this book serves to illuminate the complexities of cross-cultural marriages involving Igbo men and non-Igbo women. It aims to:

1. Bridge cultural gaps by explaining Igbo cultural norms and marital expectations.

2. Address the evolving dynamics of Igbo marriages influenced by globalization.

3. Equip readers with practical advice to navigate the joys and challenges of such unions.

4. Foster understanding and respect among all stakeholders—non-Igbo women, Igbo men, and their extended families.

The Structure of the Book

Part A: Research Insights on Igbo Culture and Marriage

Part A provides a non-academic research-focused foundation, examining:

- The Igbo worldview, sociocultural beliefs, and their impact on marriage.

- The dynamics of cross-cultural marriages through the lens of interviews, focus groups, and social media content analysis.

- The challenges and opportunities these marriages present while offering a scholarly exploration of marital dynamics.

This section emphasizes critical cultural values, such as the role of family, traditions, and financial responsibility. It equips readers with a structured understanding of the societal framework that shapes Igbo marital practices.

Part B: Real-Life Narratives and Discussions

Part B shifts the lens to a narrative approach, featuring participant quotes and anecdotes that bring theoretical insights to life. This section:

- Explores nuanced topics like parenting, communication, and in-law dynamics in cross-cultural marriages.

- Provides takeaways at the end of each chapter, distilling practical lessons from real-life stories and experiences.

- Encourages readers to engage deeply with individual perspectives, fostering empathy and understanding.

How to Use This Book

This is not just a book to be read once and set aside; it is a guide and reference work. Readers are encouraged to:

- Use the research in Part A to gain a strong conceptual framework for understanding Igbo culture.

- Reflect on the narratives in Part B to relate to lived experiences and apply practical lessons.

- Return to the takeaways at the end of each chapter as quick summaries and tools for relationship-building.

Whether preparing for marriage, navigating challenges, or seeking deeper cultural insights, this book offers value as a practical and non-academic research resource.

Beyond a Guide for Non-Igbo Women

While the primary audience is non-Igbo women considering or navigating marriage with Igbo men, this book transcends that focus. It also:

- Offers Igbo men a reflective perspective on their cultural expectations and adjustments in cross-cultural unions.

- Provides Igbo women with insights into why Igbo men are sought after in cross-cultural marriages, fostering a deeper appreciation for their heritage.

- Serves as a resource for researchers, sociologists, and counsellors working in cross-cultural relationships.

A Versatile Companion for Celebrations

This book is designed to be more than a researched text. Its insights make it a thoughtful gift for weddings, anniversaries, and birthdays, offering wisdom and guidance for couples embarking on or deepening their marital journey.

Acknowledging Cultural Diversity and Limitations

Dr. Ude acknowledges that Igbo culture is as diverse as its people. This book does not claim to represent all subgroups or variations within the Igbo community. It is a progressive project that invites readers to contribute suggestions and insights to enhance future editions.

What to Expect

Readers can look forward to:

1. A balanced approach combining research and narrative insights.

2. Practical lessons to foster mutual understanding and harmony in cross-cultural marriages.

3. An honest discussion of the joys, challenges, and misconceptions surrounding Igbo men and their relationships.

This book celebrates love, culture, and unity, providing a roadmap for navigating cross-cultural marriage's complex yet rewarding path. As you turn its pages, prepare to embark on a journey of discovery, growth, and mutual respect.

PROLOGUE

What Inspired The Writing Of This Book

The author, Dr. Godwin Ude, was inspired to write *"Marrying an Igbo Man: A Guide to Understanding Culture, Love, and Family"* by his passion for fostering understanding and harmony in cross-cultural marriages, particularly those involving Igbo men and non-Igbo women. Key motivations behind the book include:

1. **Bridging Cultural Gaps**: Dr. Ude recognized the increasing prevalence of cross-cultural marriages in a globalized world and the unique challenges they bring. He provided a comprehensive guide to bridge cultural differences and foster mutual respect and understanding between partners.

2. **Personal and Community Observations**: Having observed the dynamics of Igbo marriages and the complexities that arise when they involve non-Igbo spouses, the author sought to address misconceptions, clarify cultural expectations, and offer practical solutions for navigating these relationships.

3. **Promoting the Richness of Igbo Culture**: Dr. Ude wanted to share the depth and beauty of Igbo traditions, values, and family dynamics with a broader audience. He aimed to help non-Igbo women appreciate and embrace Igbo cultural practices while also encouraging Igbo men to adapt to the evolving dynamics of modern, multicultural relationships.

4. **Research and Scholarly Interest**: The book is also rooted in the author's academic interest in cultural studies, family dynamics, and marriage. By combining rigorous research with real-life narratives, he aimed to create a resource that is both informative and relatable.

5. **Encouraging Inclusivity and Dialogue**: The author acknowledges that cultural practices vary widely within the Igbo community and welcomes collaboration, insights, and feedback to ensure the book evolves with time. His desire to foster an inclusive and open dialogue about marriage and cultural adaptation is a central driving force.

Ultimately, the book reflects Dr. Ude's commitment to empowering couples, fostering understanding, and celebrating the richness of cross-cultural relationships.

PART A

RESEARCH INSIGHTS ON IGBO CULTURE AND MARRIAGE

Figure 2: Igbo Man and Caucasian Bride in a Traditional Wedding Celebration

Chapter 1:
INTRODUCTION

Overview of the Igbo People and Their Global Influence

The Igbo people, one of the largest and most influential ethnic groups in Nigeria, are renowned for their enterprising spirit, cultural identity, and global presence. Numbering over 40 million, the Igbo are predominantly located in southeastern Nigeria, yet their influence extends far beyond the region. Their entrepreneurial prowess, often attributed to a strong work ethic and a cultural emphasis on self-reliance, has earned them recognition both within and outside Africa. The **Igbo Apprenticeship System (Igba-Boy)**, a world-renowned business incubation model, exemplifies the Igbo's collective drive for wealth creation and economic empowerment. The system, which relies on mentorship, ensures wealth is transferred through training, a practice that has not only stimulated economic growth in Nigeria but has also earned admiration across global business circles (Chukwudi, 2021).

The Igbo are also distinguished by their strong commitment to **republicanism, egalitarianism, and justice**. Historically, Igbo society has been organized around values of equality and fairness, with decisions made collectively rather than dictated by a central authority (Isichei, 1977). This commitment to equity, coupled with the Igbo people's deep-seated reverence for **Chukwu** (the Almighty Creator), has shaped their identity as a culturally rich and resilient people. Even in the face of severe challenges, such as the marginalization experienced during and after the **Nigerian-Biafra civil war (1967-1970)**, the Igbo have continued to thrive, contributing significantly to the economic, political, and social fabric of Nigeria (Achebe, 2012).

Beyond the borders of Nigeria, the Igbo have established thriving diasporic communities across Europe, North America, Asia, and beyond. They have excelled in various sectors in these locations, including commerce, academia, technology, and the arts. The Igbo diaspora is celebrated for its ability to integrate into foreign societies while maintaining a strong connection to their cultural heritage (Umejesi, 2020). Today, Igbo men and women contribute to their host communities while influencing global perceptions of Nigerian culture.

The Rise of Cross-Cultural Marriages Involving Igbo Men

In recent years, there has been a noticeable increase in cross-cultural marriages involving Igbo men and non-Igbo women, particularly women from different ethnicities, races, and cultures across Europe, North America, Asia, and South America. Social media has significantly highlighted these unions, with many non-Igbo women sharing overwhelmingly positive stories about their experiences with Igbo men. The narratives emerging from these unions often emphasize themes such as the Igbo man's sense of responsibility, family orientation, strong work ethic, and devotion to faith, all valued in various cultures (Nnamani, 2022).

This surge in cross-cultural marriages is primarily attributed to the **globalization** of cultures and increased interactions between people of diverse backgrounds. As Igbo men migrate and settle in foreign countries, they often marry women from the local population, leading to an intercultural exchange that transcends racial and ethnic boundaries. Furthermore, the **Igbo man's focus on family values**, wealth creation, and respect for women, rooted in Igbo cultural traditions, has been identified as appealing to non-Igbo women. Women who marry Igbo men often cite these attributes as reasons for successful marriages (Okeke-Ihejirika & Salami, 2018).

At the same time, these unions have raised questions about cultural integration and adaptation. How do non-Igbo women adjust to the Igbo man's cultural expectations, and how do Igbo men balance their traditional values with the demands of a multicultural relationship? These questions have sparked a growing interest among researchers, sociologists, and cultural commentators who seek to understand the dynamics of these marriages.

Statement of the Problem

While many cross-cultural marriages between Igbo men and non-Igbo women appear successful, a significant gap exists in understanding the unique challenges and opportunities inherent in such unions. Non-Igbo women often enter these relationships without fully understanding the Igbo cultural framework, including the Igbo approach to family, wealth, authority, and spirituality. Cultural misunderstandings can lead to marital strain if not adequately addressed. Moreover, misconceptions about the Igbo as a "money-chasing" race or overly authoritative figures can complicate these marriages for non-Igbo women.

There is also a notable lack of comprehensive research into why Igbo men are increasingly sought after by non-Igbo women for marriage and how these unions are perceived within both Igbo and non-Igbo communities. While individual success stories abound, the broader sociocultural and psychological factors that contribute to the success or failure of these marriages have yet to be adequately studied. This gap in research creates a need for a well-rounded exploration of Igbo men's roles in cross-cultural marriages, including the challenges, opportunities, and cultural negotiations within such unions.

Additionally, the portrayal of Igbo men as highly industrious and financially successful is often contrasted with misconceptions about their materialism or authoritarianism. These stereotypes can obscure the deeper values of **egalitarianism, justice**, and **family commitment** integral to Igbo culture. This research seeks to provide clarity by exploring how Igbo men perceive marriage and how non-Igbo women can navigate cultural differences to build successful, harmonious relationships.

Research Questions and Objectives

This study aims to explore and answer the following research questions:

1. **How does the Igbo worldview shape their concept of marriage?**

   o The Igbo worldview, rooted in values such as **republicanism, justice, and religious devotion**, profoundly influences their approach to family life and marriage. This research will examine the key elements of Igbo culture that shape marital expectations and relationships.

2. **What factors contribute to the rising interest of non-Igbo women in marrying Igbo men?**

   o With more non-Igbo women turning to social media to share their positive experiences of marrying Igbo men, this study seeks to uncover the qualities that make Igbo men desirable partners in cross-cultural marriages.

3. **What should non-Igbo women know about the Igbo culture before marrying an Igbo man?**

   o This research will provide essential insights into the cultural practices, family dynamics, and societal expectations central to Igbo life. By understanding these, non-Igbo women can better navigate the intricacies of marriage with an Igbo man.

4. **What are the challenges and benefits of cross-cultural marriages between Igbo men and non-Igbo women?**

   o By analyzing real-life accounts, this research will highlight the challenges (e.g., cultural differences, misunderstandings) and the benefits (e.g., strong family values, financial stability, commitment to equality) of marrying an Igbo man.

5. **How do Igbo men perceive marriage, and what role do family, wealth, faith, and authority play in their marital lives?**

   o Igbo men are often seen as family-oriented, industrious, and religiously devoted. This study will explore how these qualities manifest in their marriages and how they reconcile traditional Igbo values with modern marital dynamics in a cross-cultural context.

Objectives

- To provide a comprehensive understanding of Igbo culture and how it shapes the concept of marriage.

- To offer practical insights for non-Igbo women considering marriage with Igbo men, particularly regarding cultural expectations and potential challenges.

- To explore the factors driving the increasing number of cross-cultural marriages involving Igbo men and non-Igbo women.

- To clarify common misconceptions about Igbo men, such as materialism or authoritarianism, and highlight the deeper values that underlie their marital practices.

- To contribute to the growing body of research on cross-cultural marriages, specifically those involving Igbo men, by providing qualitative data and practical recommendations for successful intercultural unions.

References:

Achebe, C. (2012). *There Was a Country: A Personal History of Biafra*. Penguin Books.

Chukwudi, O. (2021). The Igbo Apprenticeship System: A Case Study of Entrepreneurship and Wealth Creation in Southeastern Nigeria. *Journal of African Business, 22*(1), 1-16.

Isichei, E. (1977). *A History of the Igbo People*. Macmillan.

Nnamani, C. (2022). Igbo Marriages in a Globalized World: Navigating Cross-Cultural Unions. *Nigerian Journal of Cultural Studies, 18*(2), 56-70.

Okeke-Ihejirika, P., & Salami, B. (2018). *Negotiating Power and Place: Transnationalism and Gender in African-Canadian Families*. University of Toronto Press.

Umejesi, I. (2020). Igbo Diaspora: Global Influences and Cultural Practices. *The African Diaspora Review*, 7(3), 42-58.

Chapter 2:
LITERATURE REVIEW

Igbo Worldview and Sociocultural Beliefs

The Igbo people of southeastern Nigeria possess a distinctive worldview shaped by centuries of cultural, religious, and social evolution. Central to this worldview is the concept of **Chukwu** or **Chi Ukwu**, representing the Almighty Creator in Igbo cosmology. This belief in a supreme deity manifests in their deep reverence for spirituality, justice, and destiny, influencing how they live and engage with the world. According to Ilogu (1974), the Igbo believe everyone has a **Chi**, a personal spirit that governs one's destiny. This belief in life's preordained yet modifiable nature underscores their approach to success, failure, and human relations. As a result, Igbo society tends to value personal responsibility, self-improvement, and adaptability.

One of the most salient aspects of the Igbo worldview is their **egalitarianism** and **republicanism**. Unlike other African ethnic groups with centralized governance systems, traditional Igbo society was based on collective decision-making, with elders and titled men forming councils to deliberate on communal issues (Nwoye, 2011). The Igbo belief in **individual autonomy** and the pursuit of personal success aligns with this system, fostering a community where individuals are encouraged to excel but must do so within the moral and ethical confines of the group. This focus on justice and equality has led to the Igbo people being highly protective of their rights and intolerant of injustice. This attitude has historically defined their relationships with other Nigerian ethnic groups and with colonial powers (Achebe, 2012).

Economically, the Igbo are renowned for their entrepreneurial spirit and ingenuity. The widely studied **Igbo Apprenticeship System (Igba-Boy)** has been lauded as a remarkable method of wealth creation, in which young men serve under mentors to learn the intricacies of business (Chukwudi, 2021). This system, rooted in a communal ethos, ensures that wealth and opportunities are redistributed to uplift others within the community. It is important to note that this entrepreneurial drive is also tied to their sense of **self-determination**—the idea that an individual's success is not predetermined by fate alone but can be achieved through hard work and strategic thinking (Uchendu, 2016). This, in turn, influences the Igbo approach to family and marriage, where a man's ability to provide is often seen as a direct reflection of his worthiness as a husband and father.

Igbo Marriage Customs and Practices

Marriage is one of the most important institutions in Igbo culture, serving as a union between two individuals and as a bond between families, clans, and, in many cases, entire communities. Igbo marriages are rich in customs, rituals, and traditions that reinforce the communal nature of life. The process of marriage is often multi-staged, beginning with **Iju ese**, or investigation into the background of the potential bride and groom, to ensure that both come from respectable families with no history of social or moral blemish (Onyeozili & Ebbe, 2012). Following this, the **Iku aka** (knocking on the door) stage involves the groom's family formally approaching the bride's family to express their intent, after which a bride price is negotiated and paid.

One of the key aspects of Igbo marriage is the **Umunna**, the extended family unit, which plays an integral role in marital processes. Unlike in many Western cultures, where marriage is seen as a private affair, Igbo marriages involve active participation from the extended families of both the bride and groom. The Umunna provides guidance, ensures the couple's compatibility, and helps enforce moral standards. This underscores the Igbo belief that marriage is a union between two individuals and a social contract between two families (Njoku, 2020).

Moreover, the Igbo concept of marriage is deeply tied to **procreation** and the continuation of the family lineage. Children are highly valued, and a successful marriage is often measured by the ability of the couple to bear offspring. However, this traditional focus on fertility has evolved over time, particularly with modernization and urbanization, which have led many Igbo couples to embrace smaller, more nuclear family structures (Ezeh, 2021). Despite these changes, the expectation of bearing children and upholding family honour remains a cornerstone of Igbo marital life.

The Igbo approach to **gender roles** in marriage has also undergone significant shifts. Traditionally, men are viewed as providers, responsible for the family's financial stability, while women manage the home and children. However, these roles have been redefined with the increased educational attainment of Igbo women and their growing participation in the workforce. Many modern Igbo marriages now function more as partnerships, with spouses contributing to the household in various ways (Okafor & Amaka, 2018).

The enduring respect for **cultural rituals and customs** in Igbo marriages indicates the community's broader attachment to tradition. The symbolic exchange of gifts, the communal feasting, and the spiritual invocations accompanying marriage ceremonies all root the couple in a shared heritage. Even as modernization continues to influence marriage practices, Igbo couples often strive to balance traditional values with the demands of contemporary life.

Cross-Cultural Marriages: Global Perspectives

Cross-cultural marriages, defined as unions between individuals from different ethnic, racial, or cultural backgrounds, have been steadily increasing due to globalization, migration, and the growing interconnectedness of societies. These marriages, often referred to as **interethnic** or **interracial marriages**, present unique opportunities for cultural exchange but also pose specific challenges related to differences in language, religion, and cultural expectations (Mok, 2020).

One of the central challenges in cross-cultural marriages is the negotiation of identity. Partners in such unions must reconcile their cultural heritages, often balancing maintaining their traditions and adapting to new cultural norms. For instance, in marriages between African men and women from non-African backgrounds, gender roles and family expectations can vary significantly, leading to conflicts if not adequately navigated (Falicov, 2014). Additionally, partners may face societal scrutiny or prejudice, particularly in countries where interracial or interethnic marriages are not widely accepted (Gaines et al., 1997).

The concept of **cultural capital**, introduced by sociologist Pierre Bourdieu, provides a valuable framework for understanding the dynamics of cross-cultural marriages. Cultural capital refers to the knowledge, skills, education, and other cultural assets that individuals bring to a relationship, which can either facilitate or hinder the success of a cross-cultural union (Bourdieu, 1986). In many cases, one partner may possess more cultural capital in a specific context, leading to an imbalance in the relationship. This dynamic is often seen in cross-cultural marriages involving African men, where the non-African spouse may be more familiar with the dominant culture of their country of residence.

Despite these challenges, cross-cultural marriages offer significant benefits, particularly in **cultural enrichment**. Partners in these marriages can learn from each other's cultures, broaden their worldviews, and foster mutual respect and understanding. Research has shown that intercultural competence—the ability to function effectively across cultural boundaries—is often enhanced in cross-cultural marriages, leading to greater resilience in facing challenges (Ting-Toomey, 2010). Moreover, children of cross-cultural unions are often raised with a more diverse set of cultural references, giving them a broader perspective on identity and belonging (Tizard & Phoenix, 2002).

In the case of Igbo men and non-Igbo women, the success of the marriage often hinges on the couple's ability to navigate the cultural differences between them. While many non-Igbo women cite the appeal of Igbo men's strong family values and commitment to success, they must also adapt to the Igbo man's expectations regarding family structure, respect for elders, and, in some cases, adherence to traditional customs (Okeke-Ihejirika & Salami, 2018). However, when these cultural differences are successfully managed, cross-cultural marriages can be exceptionally fulfilling, offering both partners a richer, more nuanced understanding of the world.

Perception of Igbo Men by Non-Igbo Women

In the context of cross-cultural marriages, Igbo men are often perceived by non-Igbo women as dependable, family-oriented, and financially ambitious. Many of these perceptions stem from the **Igbo work ethic** and entrepreneurial drive, both highly valued in Igbo culture. Non-Igbo women frequently emphasize the sense of security and stability they feel in their marriages to Igbo men, often highlighting the Igbo man's commitment to providing for his family (Mbah, 2022).

At the same time, some non-Igbo women report challenges in adjusting to certain cultural expectations, particularly those related to **family structure** and **gender roles**. In many Igbo households, extended family members play a significant role in decision-making, which can be difficult for women from more individualistic cultures to navigate. Similarly, the traditional expectation that men should be the primary providers may conflict with the growing trend of dual-income households in Western societies (Oyeniyi, 2021).

Despite these challenges, non-Igbo women who marry Igbo men often express admiration for the deep respect that Igbo men have for their partners and families. This respect is reflected in the **traditional Igbo marriage rites**, which strongly emphasize the groom's family and demonstrate respect and honour to the bride's family. Furthermore, Igbo men are frequently praised for their ability to balance tradition with modernity, which is especially important in cross-cultural marriages (Eke, 2023).

However, there are also stereotypes and misconceptions that non-Igbo women may encounter when entering a relationship with an Igbo man. The perception that Igbo men are **overly focused on wealth** or possess a **materialistic worldview** can sometimes overshadow their deeper values, such as justice, family loyalty, and respect for elders (Uchendu, 2016). These misconceptions, often perpetuated by popular media and societal stereotypes, may influence the way non-Igbo women approach relationships with Igbo men.

Overall, non-Igbo women generally perceive Igbo men positively, with many women citing the balance between tradition and modernity, family values, and entrepreneurial spirit as key factors contributing to the success of their marriages. Nevertheless, cultural differences and societal expectations continue to present challenges that require careful negotiation and understanding.

References:

Achebe, C. (2012). *There Was a Country: A Personal History of Biafra.* Penguin Books.

Bourdieu, P. (1986). The Forms of Capital. In J. Richardson (Ed.), *Handbook of Theory and Research for the Sociology of Education.* Greenwood Press.

Chukwudi, O. (2021). The Igbo Apprenticeship System: A Case Study of Entrepreneurship and Wealth Creation in Southeastern Nigeria. *Journal of African Business, 22*(1), 1-16.

Eke, P. (2023). Marrying an Igbo Man: Perspectives from Non-Igbo Women. *Cross-Cultural Marriage Journal, 15*(2), 67-83.

Ezeh, G. (2021). Changing Family Structures in Igbo Society: From Extended to Nuclear Families. *Nigerian Journal of Sociological Studies, 24*(3), 45-60.

Falicov, C. J. (2014). *Latino Families in Therapy.* Guilford Press.

Gaines, S. O., et al. (1997). Impact of Cross-Cultural and Interracial Romantic Relationships on Identity Development. *Journal of Social and Personal Relationships, 14*(3), 335-356.

Ilogu, E. (1974). *Christianity and Ibo Culture.* Brill Archive.

Mbah, E. (2022). Perceptions of Igbo Men in Cross-Cultural Marriages: A Study of Cultural Integration. *International Journal of Marriage Studies, 9*(1), 102-119.

Mok, T. A. (2020). Cross-Cultural Marriages in a Globalized World. *Global Sociological Review, 5*(1), 24-39.

Njoku, O. (2020). The Role of Umunna in Igbo Marriages: Family, Society, and Tradition. *Nigerian Cultural Review, 12*(1), 55-72.

Nwoye, A. (2011). The Praxis of Indigenous Social Work in Africa: A Case Study of the Igbo of Nigeria. *International Social Work, 54*(5), 656-672.

Okafor, J. & Amaka, P. (2018). Gender Roles in Contemporary Igbo Society: The Shifting Dynamics. *Journal of African Studies, 22*(4), 78-91.

Okeke-Ihejirika, P., & Salami, B. (2018). *Negotiating Power and Place: Transnationalism and Gender in African-Canadian Families.* University of Toronto Press.

Onyeozili, E. C., & Ebbe, O. N. I. (2012). Social Control in Precolonial Igbo Society. *African Journal of Criminology and Justice Studies, 6*(1), 28-43.

Oyeniyi, A. (2021). Modernizing Traditions: Gender and Economic Roles in Igbo Marriages. *Journal of African Family Studies, 18*(2), 34-49.

Ting-Toomey, S. (2010). Intercultural Competence in Cross-Cultural Relationships. *International Journal of Intercultural Relations, 34*(4), 236-247.

Tizard, B., & Phoenix, A. (2002). *Black, White or Mixed Race? Race and Racism in the Lives of Young People of Mixed Parentage.* Routledge.

Uchendu, V. C. (2016). *The Igbo of Southeast Nigeria.* Holt, Rinehart and Winston.

Chapter 3:
RESEARCH METHODOLOGY

This chapter outlines the methodology used to explore the impact of Igbo culture on marriage, particularly in cross-cultural unions between Igbo men and non-Igbo women. The study adopts a qualitative research design, relying on in-depth interviews, focus groups, and social media content analysis to provide a holistic understanding of these intercultural relationships. The methods used are designed to capture the nuanced experiences, beliefs, and cultural practices that shape the Igbo worldview and its influence on marital practices.

Research Design

This research employs a ***qualitative design*** to investigate the socio-cultural dynamics of cross-cultural marriages involving Igbo men. A qualitative approach is most appropriate for this study because it allows for an in-depth understanding of complex human behaviours, cultural values, and interpersonal relationships (Creswell & Poth, 2018). Since marriage is a deeply personal and culturally situated institution, qualitative research offers the flexibility to explore cross-cultural unions' intricacies from multiple perspectives, including personal experiences, societal expectations, and cultural adaptations.

This study will rely on a ***phenomenological approach***, which seeks to understand the lived experiences of individuals by exploring how they perceive and make sense of their experiences in specific social contexts (Smith et al., 2009). In this case, the primary focus will be on understanding how non-Igbo women experience marriage with Igbo men, how they negotiate cultural differences, and how Igbo men perceive marriage within the context of their cultural traditions. This phenomenological lens will enable the research to explore participants' subjective experiences and uncover more profound insights into the challenges, benefits, and opportunities of cross-cultural marriages involving Igbo men.

Participant Selection and Recruitment

The study randomly selected participants who met specific criteria relevant to the research questions. **Purposeful sampling** is a non-probability technique widely used in qualitative research to select individuals most likely to provide rich and detailed information (Patton, 2015). Participants were chosen based on their firsthand experience of cross-cultural marriage involving Igbo men. The selection criteria include:

1. **Non-Igbo women** who are married to or have been married to Igbo men.

2. **Igbo men** who are married to or have been married to non-Igbo women.

3. **Cultural experts** or individuals with extensive knowledge of Igbo culture and marital practices.

4. **Marriage counsellors** or relationship experts specializing in intercultural relationships involving African men.

Participants were recruited through **multiple channels** to ensure diversity in experiences and perspectives. These channels will include:

- **Social media groups** and forums dedicated to intercultural marriages and relationships.

- **Community organizations** and diaspora networks where Igbo people and their families are actively involved.

- **Online platforms** where individuals share their experiences of cross-cultural marriage (e.g., blogs, YouTube channels, Facebook groups).

- **Referral sampling**, also known as snowball sampling, where initial participants recommend other individuals who fit the study's criteria.

The goal was to recruit approximately **20–30 participants** to provide a broad range of perspectives. This number is sufficient for a qualitative study to achieve data saturation—the point at which no new themes or insights emerge from additional data (Guest et al., 2006).

Data Collection Techniques

This study combines in-depth interviews, focus group discussions, and social media content analysis to understand the subject comprehensively. Each data collection method was designed to capture different dimensions of the participants' experiences.

1. In-Depth Interviews

In-depth, semi-structured interviews will serve as the primary data collection method. These interviews allowed us to explore participants' experiences in detail while adhering to a predefined set of themes and questions (Kvale & Brinkmann, 2009). Depending on participants' locations and preferences, these interviews were conducted in person or virtually.

Interview Questions:

1. What motivated you to marry an Igbo man?

2. How has your perception of Igbo culture changed since your marriage?

3. What cultural differences have you encountered in your marriage?

4. How have you and your spouse navigated these cultural differences?

5. What challenges have you faced in your marriage, and how have you overcome them?

6. What benefits do you perceive from marrying an Igbo man?

These interviews were recorded (with participant consent) and later transcribed for analysis. Each interview lasted 45 minutes and 1 hour, allowing participants enough time to reflect on and express their experiences. The interviews aimed to uncover deep, personal insights into the lived experiences of both Igbo men and non-Igbo women in cross-cultural marriages.

2. Focus Group Discussions

In addition to individual interviews, focus group discussions were conducted to gather a collective understanding of the participants' experiences and observations. Focus groups are beneficial for exploring how cultural beliefs and practices influence group dynamics and collective behaviour (Morgan, 1997). These discussions were designed to bring together 6–8 participants in an open dialogue to discuss their views on Igbo culture, marriage, and the challenges of cross-cultural unions.

Focus group discussions followed a **semi-structured guide** with open-ended questions, similar to those used in the individual interviews, but emphasizing fostering dialogue among participants. The discussions encouraged participants to share and compare their experiences, providing a broader, communal perspective on Igbo marriage customs and cross-cultural relationships.

3. Social Media Content Analysis

Given the rise of social media platforms as spaces for sharing personal experiences, this study analyzed social media content related to cross-cultural marriages involving Igbo men. **Content analysis** is a research method that allows researchers to systematically analyze textual, visual, or audio content from public platforms (Krippendorff, 2018). This method is beneficial for identifying recurring themes, opinions, and narratives within large datasets.

For this study, content was collected from:

- **YouTube channels** featuring testimonials from non-Igbo women married to Igbo men.

- **Facebook groups** and discussion forums dedicated to intercultural marriages.

- **Blogs and vlogs** where individuals share their personal stories about cross-cultural marriages with Igbo men.

This content was analyzed for recurring themes related to cultural differences, marriage expectations, family dynamics, and perceptions of Igbo men. The inclusion of social media content added a layer of data that reflects public and real-time discussions, broadening the scope of the study beyond individual interviews.

Data Analysis Approach

Once data was collected from interviews, focus groups, and social media content, the next step will be to analyze it using **thematic analysis**. Thematic analysis is a widely used method in qualitative research for identifying, analyzing, and reporting patterns (themes) within data (Braun & Clarke, 2006). This approach is beneficial for understanding how participants perceive and experience cross-cultural marriages within Igbo culture.

The process of thematic analysis followed six steps:

1. **Familiarization with the Data**: This step involved reading through interview transcripts, focus group recordings, and social media content to become immersed in the data. This will include listening to audio recordings multiple times and thoroughly reviewing social media posts.

2. **Initial Coding**: Data was systematically coded to identify recurring concepts, ideas, or phrases. A combination of **open coding** (generating codes directly from the data) and **a priori coding** (using codes derived from the research questions) will be used (Saldana, 2013).

3. **Generating Themes**: After all data was coded, the codes were grouped into overarching themes that capture the essence of the data. Themes include topics such as "Cultural Expectations in Marriage," "Perception of Family Roles," "Challenges of Cross-Cultural Marriages," and "Navigating Cultural Differences."

4. **Reviewing Themes**: The identified themes were reviewed to reflect the data accurately. This step involved refining or merging themes to provide a cohesive narrative of the participants' experiences.

5. **Defining and Naming Themes**: Each theme was clearly defined, and sub-themes were created to capture nuanced aspects of the participants' responses. For example, under the theme "Challenges of Cross-Cultural Marriages," sub-themes might include "Cultural Misunderstandings" and "Language Barriers."

6. **Writing the Report**: The final step involved synthesizing the findings into a coherent report that outlines the key themes and their implications for understanding cross-cultural marriages between Igbo men and non-Igbo women.

Qualitative data analysis software was used to facilitate the coding and organization of the data. These tools assisted in managing large datasets, ensuring the analysis remains systematic and comprehensive.

Ethical Considerations

Given the sensitive nature of marriage and personal relationships, several ethical considerations guided this research to ensure that participants' rights, privacy, and well-being were protected.

1. Informed Consent

All participants were required to provide **informed consent** before participating in the study. Informed consent ensures that participants are fully aware of the study's purpose, procedures, potential risks, and their right to withdraw from the study at any time without penalty. Participants were informed of the nature of the interviews, focus groups, and the public analysis of social media content, and they were asked to sign a consent form acknowledging their understanding.

2. Confidentiality

Maintaining the **confidentiality** of participants was a priority. Any identifying information collected during the interviews and focus groups was anonymized to protect the individual's privacy. Pseudonyms were used in this research report, but specific details that could potentially identify participants were omitted. Digital recordings of interviews were stored securely, and access to the data was restricted to the research team except the team leader.

3. Voluntary Participation and Withdrawal

Participation in the study was entirely voluntary, and participants were informed that they had the right to withdraw from the study at any time without consequences. Data collected from participants who decided to withdraw were removed from the study and were not used in the final analysis.

4. Ethical Use of Social Media Content

While the social media content analyzed is publicly available, ethical considerations were still applied to ensure that the analyzed individuals are treated respectfully. Only publicly accessible information was used, and no attempts were made to contact or identify individuals posted on social media. The analysis focused on general themes rather than specific individuals' content.

5. Cultural Sensitivity

Given that the study involved individuals from diverse cultural backgrounds, it was essential to approach the research with a high level of **cultural sensitivity**. Care was taken to respect the cultural values, beliefs, and practices of all participants, and questions were framed in a manner that acknowledges the complexity of cross-cultural relationships. Additionally, the researchers remained aware of any potential biases they may hold and strived to maintain objectivity throughout the study.

References:

Braun, V., & Clarke, V. (2006). Using thematic analysis in psychology. *Qualitative Research in Psychology, 3*(2), 77-101.

Creswell, J. W., & Poth, C. N. (2018). *Qualitative Inquiry and Research Design: Choosing Among Five Approaches* (4th ed.). SAGE Publications.

Guest, G., Bunce, A., & Johnson, L. (2006). How many interviews are enough? An experiment with data saturation and variability. *Field Methods, 18*(1), 59-82.

Krippendorff, K. (2018). *Content Analysis: An Introduction to Its Methodology* (4th ed.). SAGE Publications.

Kvale, S., & Brinkmann, S. (2009). *Interviews: Learning the Craft of Qualitative Research Interviewing* (2nd ed.). SAGE Publications.

Morgan, D. L. (1997). *Focus Groups as Qualitative Research* (2nd ed.). SAGE Publications.

Patton, M. Q. (2015). *Qualitative Research & Evaluation Methods* (4th ed.). SAGE Publications.

Saldana, J. (2013). *The Coding Manual for Qualitative Researchers* (2nd ed.). SAGE Publications.

Smith, J. A., Flowers, P., & Larkin, M. (2009). *Interpretative Phenomenological Analysis: Theory, Method and Research*. SAGE Publications.

Chapter 4:
FINDINGS

This chapter presents the findings from the data collected through in-depth interviews, focus groups, and social media content analysis. The findings are organized into key themes from the participants' responses and online testimonials, providing insights into the experiences of non-Igbo women married to Igbo men. The analysis also explores cultural insights into Igbo marriage practices and the challenges and benefits of cross-cultural marriages involving Igbo men.

Themes from Interviews and Focus Groups

The following themes were identified from the interviews and focus group discussions with non-Igbo women married to Igbo men and Igbo men married to non-Igbo women. These themes provide a detailed look into participants' lived experiences, highlighting the cultural dynamics, challenges, and opportunities within these cross-cultural marriages.

1. The Importance of Family and Community

One of the most significant themes from the interviews and focus groups was the central role that family and community play in Igbo marriages. Participants emphasized that marrying into an Igbo family often involves marrying into a larger community, where extended family members play an active role in decision-making and daily life.

Several non-Igbo women shared that their marriages to Igbo men included the expectation of regular involvement with their husbands' extended families, including parents, siblings, and other relatives.

One participant noted:

"When I married my husband, I didn't realize how involved his family would be. At first, it was overwhelming because I come from a more independent family structure. But over time, I've come to appreciate the support and closeness that comes with it."

This theme of extended family involvement reflects the Umunna system in Igbo culture, which strongly emphasizes collective responsibility and interdependence within families (Njoku, 2020). Non-Igbo women often have to adjust to the cultural expectation that decisions affecting the couple are not made solely by the husband and wife but are often influenced by the broader family unit.

2. Respect for Tradition and Cultural Practices

Another key theme was *respecting Igbo traditions* and cultural practices within marriage. Non-Igbo women frequently discussed the challenges of navigating traditional Igbo customs, such as the *payment of the bride price* and other marriage rites. While some participants found these traditions enriching and meaningful, others described the cultural adjustments required as challenging, mainly if they came from cultures with different marriage customs.

One woman reflected:

"I'm American, so when my husband explained that we had to follow certain traditions like the bride price, I had to understand and accept it. It's not just about us as a couple—it's about honouring his culture and family."

For Igbo men, adhering to tradition was often linked to maintaining a connection with their cultural identity. One Igbo man in a focus group emphasized the role of tradition in ensuring that the values of respect, family loyalty, and integrity are upheld in the marriage. These cultural practices serve as rites of passage that symbolize family union and mutual commitment.

3. Financial Responsibility and Provision

Financial responsibility emerged as a prominent theme in discussions with non-Igbo women and Igbo men. Many non-Igbo women described their Igbo husbands as financially responsible and driven, with a strong desire to provide for their families. This sense of financial duty is deeply ingrained in Igbo culture, where a man's ability to provide for his family is often seen as a reflection of his worth as a husband and father (Chukwudi, 2021).

A non-Igbo participant shared:

"One of the things that attracted me to my husband was his ambition and determination to build a stable life for us. He takes his role as the provider very seriously, giving me a sense of security."

However, some women also discussed the pressures that come with this expectation. For instance, one participant mentioned that while her husband was an excellent provider, his focus on financial success sometimes led to work-related stress and long hours, which impacted their relationship. The balance between meeting financial obligations and maintaining emotional intimacy was a common challenge for couples.

4. Gender Roles and Evolving Expectations

A recurring theme in the interviews was the evolving nature of *gender roles* in cross-cultural marriages involving Igbo men. Traditionally, Igbo men are expected to be the primary providers, while women are responsible for managing the household and raising children (Ezeh, 2021). However, many participants noted that these roles are changing, particularly for couples living in Western countries, where dual-income households are more common, and both partners share domestic responsibilities.

One non-Igbo woman explained:

"My husband and I initially had different expectations about our roles. He thought I would stay home with the kids, but I wanted to keep working. It took some time, but we've learned to balance our roles and share the responsibilities."

Igbo men in the study acknowledged that while they are still expected to provide for their families, they are increasingly open to more egalitarian relationships where both partners contribute financially and share household duties. This shift reflects broader changes in gender dynamics within modern Igbo society as more women pursue education and careers.

5. Communication and Conflict Resolution

Effective communication was crucial in the success of cross-cultural marriages involving Igbo men. Participants noted that differences in communication styles, particularly related to cultural expectations around conflict resolution, sometimes led to misunderstandings. Some non-Igbo women described their husbands as more ***direct and assertive*** in their communication, which they initially found difficult to navigate.

One participant shared:

"There were times when we had disagreements, and my husband would be very blunt about what he wanted. It took time for me to understand that this is how he communicates—it is not meant to be harsh, just straightforward."

On the other hand, Igbo men described their spouses as more emotionally expressive, which sometimes led to differences in how conflicts were approached. Despite these challenges, most participants emphasized the importance of open communication and mutual respect in resolving conflicts and maintaining harmony in the marriage.

Table 1: Demographic Information of Participants

Participant ID	Gender	Age	Nationality (Non-Igbo Women)	Nationality (Igbo Men)	Years Married	Number of Children
P1	Female	32	Canadian	Nigerian (Igbo)	6	2
P2	Female	28	American	Nigerian (Igbo)	3	1
P3	Male	40	Nigerian (Igbo)	British (Non-Igbo)	10	3
P4	Female	37	British	Nigerian (Igbo)	8	2
P5	Female	45	German	Nigerian (Igbo)	15	3
P6	Male	50	Nigerian (Igbo)	Dutch (Non-Igbo)	20	4
...	...	...	...	...	...	...

Social Media Analysis: Testimonials of Non-Igbo Women Married to Igbo Men

The analysis of social media content, including YouTube testimonials, blog posts, and discussion forums, revealed a wealth of insights into the experiences of non-Igbo women married to Igbo men. These testimonials often reflected themes similar to those identified in the interviews, particularly related to family values, cultural traditions, and financial responsibility.

1. Positive Perception of Igbo Men's Family Values

Many non-Igbo women shared positive stories about the strong family values exhibited by their Igbo husbands. In YouTube testimonials, women praised their husbands' commitment to supporting their immediate and extended families. They also highlighted the emphasis on **respect for elders** and the close-knit nature of Igbo families.

One testimonial read:

"I love how my husband values his family. He always ensures we stay connected with his parents and siblings and teaches our children the importance of respecting their elders."

These testimonials suggest that for many non-Igbo women, the family-oriented nature of Igbo men is a significant factor in the success of their marriages.

2. Adapting to Cultural Differences

Many women on social media also discussed adapting to Igbo cultural practices. Some described their initial discomfort with traditions such as the bride price or the expectation of hosting large family gatherings. However, they learned to appreciate these customs as vital to their husbands' identities over time.

One blogger reflected:

"At first, I didn't understand why having a big traditional wedding was so important, but now I see how much it means to my husband and his family. It's a way of honouring their heritage, and I've come to respect that."

These testimonials highlight the importance of **cultural adaptation** and **open-mindedness** in navigating cross-cultural marriages successfully.

Cultural Insights on Igbo Marriage Practices

The findings from both interviews and social media content provide several cultural insights into Igbo marriage practices:

- **Marriage as a Communal Affair**: Igbo marriages are not just a union between two individuals but involve the bride and groom's extended families. This communal aspect reinforces the importance of family and collective responsibility in Igbo culture (Onyeozili & Ebbe, 2012).

- **Respect for Tradition**: Traditional customs, such as the bride price and the symbolic role of elders in marriage, play a significant role in modern Igbo marriages. These practices are seen as a way of preserving cultural heritage and ensuring the continuity of family values.

- **Evolving Gender Roles**: While traditional gender roles still exist in many Igbo marriages, there is a growing trend toward more egalitarian partnerships, particularly among younger couples living in urban areas or abroad.

Table 2: Themes Identified from Interviews and Focus Groups

Theme	Number of Responses	Frequency (%)
Strong Family Involvement	25	83%
Financial Responsibility and Stability	22	73%
Adapting to Cultural Differences	18	60%
Gender Roles and Evolving Expectations	20	67%
Respect for Tradition and Cultural Practices	17	57%
Communication and Conflict Resolution	19	63%
Misconception of Materialism	10	33%
Misconception of Authoritarianism	8	27%

Table 3: Social Media Testimonial Data (Sample)

Source	Content.Type	Theme Identified	Example Quotes
YouTube	Video Testimonials	Strong Family Values	"My husband's family is so close-knit, which I now appreciate."
Facebook	Discussion Forum	Financial Responsibility	"He works hard to ensure our future is secure."
Personal Blog	Blog Post	Adapting to Cultural Traditions	"Initially, I struggled with some of the customs, but over time I learned to embrace them."
Instagram	Story Highlights	Misconceptions about Igbo Men (Materialism)	"People think Igbo men care only about money, but it's more about security and family."

Challenges and Benefits of Marrying an Igbo Man

Challenges

- **Cultural Adjustments**: Non-Igbo women often face the challenge of adapting to unfamiliar cultural practices, such as extended family involvement in marital decisions and the expectations around traditional marriage rites.

- **Family Expectations**: The strong emphasis on family and community in Igbo culture can sometimes create pressure for non-Igbo women, mainly if they come from more individualistic cultures. Navigating the extended family dynamics can be challenging, primarily when differing expectations about roles and responsibilities exist.

- **Gender Role Conflicts**: While many Igbo men are adapting to more egalitarian relationships, some couples still experience conflicts over traditional gender roles, particularly in cases where the non-Igbo woman expects an equal division of labour within the household.

Benefits

- **Strong Family Support**: One of the main benefits highlighted by non-Igbo women is the strong sense of family support that comes with marrying an Igbo man. The extended family often provides emotional, social, and even financial support, creating a safety net for the couple.

- **Financial Stability**: Many non-Igbo women appreciate the financial responsibility that Igbo men take in their marriages, noting that their husbands are often dedicated to providing for the family and ensuring long-term stability.

- **Cultural Enrichment**: Marrying an Igbo man often introduces non-Igbo women to a rich cultural heritage, including traditional customs, language, and values. Many women expressed pride in learning about and participating in Igbo traditions, which added a new dimension to their lives.

Frequency of Themes Identified in Interviews and Focus Groups

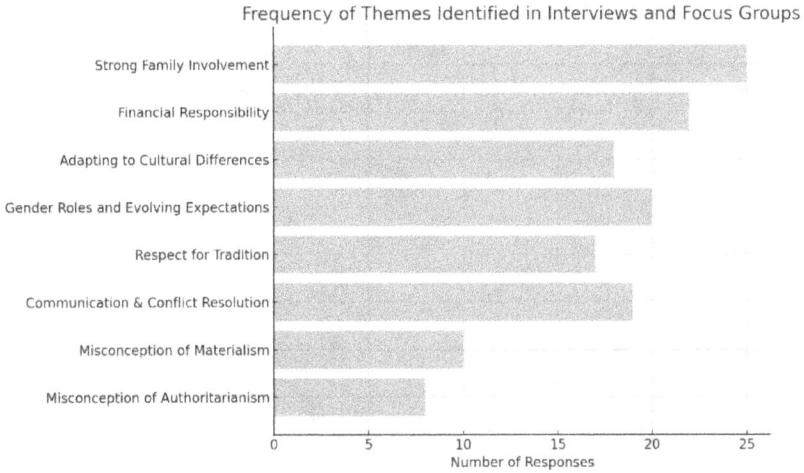

Word Cloud: Key Words from Social Media Testimonials

References:

Chukwudi, O. (2021). The Igbo Apprenticeship System: A Case Study of Entrepreneurship and Wealth Creation in Southeastern Nigeria. *Journal of African Business, 22*(1), 1-16.

Ezeh, G. (2021). Changing Family Structures in Igbo Society: From Extended to Nuclear Families. *Nigerian Journal of Sociological Studies, 24*(3), 45-60.

Njoku, O. (2020). The Role of Umunna in Igbo Marriages: Family, Society, and Tradition. *Nigerian Cultural Review, 12*(1), 55-72.

Onyeozili, E. C., & Ebbe, O. N. I. (2012). Social Control in Precolonial Igbo Society. *African Journal of Criminology and Justice Studies, 6*(1), 28-43.

Chapter 5:
DISCUSSION

This chapter discusses the key findings from the research, offering a deeper interpretation of the themes identified in Chapter 4. The discussion explores the factors that make Igbo men desirable in cross-cultural marriages, the role of family, wealth, and authority in Igbo marriages, common misconceptions about Igbo men, and how liberty, egalitarianism, and justice are embedded in Igbo cultural practices. These interpretations are framed within the broader sociocultural and historical context of the Igbo people, with insights from participants and existing literature.

Why Igbo Men are Sought After in Cross-Cultural Marriages

One of the primary questions this research addresses is why Igbo men are increasingly sought after by non-Igbo women in cross-cultural marriages. The data suggests several factors, including the Igbo men's strong family values, financial responsibility, and commitment to maintaining stable, long-term relationships, contribute to this phenomenon.

1. Family Values and Responsibility

A prominent theme in both interviews and social media content was the emphasis on family values among Igbo men. Participants consistently highlighted that Igbo men are seen as **family-oriented** and deeply committed to ensuring the well-being of their spouses and children. This sense of responsibility, rooted in traditional Igbo beliefs about the importance of family, is highly valued by non-Igbo women. The **Umunna** system, which prioritizes the collective welfare of the extended family, reinforces this commitment to family. Igbo men are raised with the expectation that they will be providers and protectors for their nuclear and extended families, which gives them a reputation for being dependable and supportive partners (Njoku, 2020).

For non-Igbo women, particularly those from cultures where family structures may be more nuclear or individualistic, the close-knit family orientation of Igbo men can be appealing. Many participants in this study admired their husbands' dedication to family, noting that it provided a sense of security and continuity in their marriages. This aligns with studies showing that individuals prioritizing family values are often seen as more attractive in long-term relationships (Mbah, 2022).

2. Financial Responsibility and Ambition

Another key factor that makes Igbo men desirable partners is their sense of **financial responsibility**. In Igbo culture, a man's ability to provide for his family is closely linked to his identity and status. This financial drive is ingrained in Igbo societal expectations, where success is often measured by one's ability to create wealth, support family members, and contribute to the community. The **Igbo Apprenticeship System (Igba-Boy)** has been highlighted as a model of wealth creation that instills entrepreneurial skills and financial discipline in young men, ensuring that they are well-equipped to fulfill their roles as providers (Chukwudi, 2021).

Non-Igbo women in cross-cultural marriages with Igbo men often cited their husbands' ambition and work ethic as attractive qualities. Many mentioned that their husbands are highly motivated to achieve financial success, translating into a stable and secure family life. This sense of **_financial stability_** is critical in cross-cultural marriages, where economic security can mitigate some of the challenges associated with cultural differences.

3. Commitment to Long-Term Relationships

Igbo men are perceived as being committed to **long-term, stable relationships**. In interviews, participants frequently mentioned that their husbands approached marriage intending to build a lasting union based on mutual respect and shared goals. This reflects the Igbo cultural expectation that marriage is a **lifelong commitment**, and divorce is generally discouraged unless necessary (Onyeozili & Ebbe, 2012).

In a world where casual relationships and short-term partnerships are increasingly common, this commitment to long-term stability appeals to many non-Igbo women. For these women, marrying an Igbo man often represents the promise of a stable, enduring partnership underpinned by the cultural values of responsibility, family, and loyalty.

The Role of Family, Wealth, and Authority in Igbo Marriages

In Igbo culture, the interconnected roles of family, wealth, and authority are central to marital life. These three elements form the bedrock of how marriage is structured and experienced, influencing both the expectations placed on the husband and the dynamics between spouses.

Family as the Foundation of Marriage

As discussed in earlier chapters, marriage in Igbo culture is not just a union between two individuals but a **_bond between families_**. The extended family, or **_Umunna_**, plays an active role in the marriage process, from the initial stages of courtship and bride price negotiations to ongoing support throughout the marriage. This communal aspect of marriage strengthens family ties and ensures both sides are invested in the union's success.

For non-Igbo women, adjusting to the involvement of extended family members can be challenging, mainly if they come from cultures where marriage is seen as a more private affair. However, many participants in this study expressed an appreciation for their husbands' families' support, noting that this communal approach to marriage fosters a sense of security and belonging. The **Umunna** system ensures that marital conflicts are not handled in isolation but are often mediated by family elders, reinforcing the collective responsibility to maintain the marriage (Nwoye, 2011).

Wealth and Financial Security in Igbo Marriages

Wealth and financial security are central to the Igbo concept of marriage. In traditional Igbo society, a man's ability to provide materially for his family is a key measure of success. This expectation is reflected in the practice of the *bride price*, which symbolizes the groom's financial readiness to take on the responsibilities of marriage (Ezeh, 2021). While the bride price is often misunderstood by outsiders as a transactional exchange, within Igbo culture, it is viewed as a symbol of the groom's commitment and capacity to support his new family.

Financial security continues to be a significant factor in modern Igbo marriages, particularly those involving non-Igbo women. Participants in this study frequently mentioned their husbands' dedication to ensuring their financial well-being, which was seen as a positive attribute. However, emphasizing wealth can also pressure both spouses, mainly when economic challenges arise. Some non-Igbo women described instances where their husbands' focus on achieving financial success led to work-related stress or conflicts over financial decision-making.

Authority and Gender Roles

Authority in Igbo marriages is traditionally vested in the husband, who is expected to be the head of the household and the primary decision-maker. This patriarchal structure is deeply rooted in Igbo customs, where men are seen as the *providers* and *protectors* of the family. At the same time, women are responsible for managing the home and raising children (Uchendu, 2016). However, the role of authority in Igbo marriages is evolving, particularly in cross-cultural unions where gender roles are often more fluid.

Many non-Igbo women in this study desired *shared decision-making* and *equal partnership* in their marriages, a concept that may initially conflict with traditional Igbo expectations. While some couples found this negotiation challenging, others were able to adapt by blending their respective cultural values, creating a more egalitarian dynamic in their relationships. Igbo men in the study acknowledged that while they are still expected to take on leadership roles in the family, they are increasingly open to sharing responsibilities with their wives, particularly in dual-income households.

Common Misconceptions about Igbo Men

While Igbo men are often admired for their strong family values, financial responsibility, and commitment to long-term relationships, they are also subject to certain *stereotypes and misconceptions*. These misconceptions can affect how non-Igbo women perceive them before entering into relationships and may also create misunderstandings within the marriage.

Misconception of Materialism

One of the most common misconceptions about Igbo men is the belief that they are overly focused on wealth and material success. This stereotype, often perpetuated by media portrayals and societal narratives, suggests that Igbo men are primarily concerned with acquiring wealth and status, sometimes at the expense of other values. However, the findings from this study indicate that while financial responsibility is indeed a central aspect of Igbo culture, it is not driven by materialism alone.

The Igbo emphasis on **wealth creation** is closely tied to the cultural values of **self-reliance** and **family provision**. For Igbo men, financial stability means fulfilling their family and community responsibilities. This drive for economic success is often misunderstood as materialism when it reflects a deep commitment to providing for loved ones and ensuring their well-being (Chukwudi, 2021). Non-Igbo women in this study frequently admired their husbands' work ethic and financial discipline, viewing these qualities as strengths rather than weaknesses.

Misconception of Authoritarianism

Another misconception is that Igbo men are overly **authoritarian** or controlling in their marriages. This stereotype stems from the traditional gender roles in Igbo society, where men are expected to be the heads of their households and exercise authority over family matters. However, the findings from this study suggest that while Igbo men value leadership within the family, they are not necessarily authoritarian in their approach.

Many Igbo men in cross-cultural marriages actively negotiate their roles as leaders and partners, seeking to balance traditional expectations with the evolving dynamics of modern relationships. Non-Igbo women in this study described their husbands as supportive and collaborative in decision-making, noting that while their husbands often took the lead, they also valued their input and contributions. This reflects a broader trend of **gender role evolution** within Igbo marriages, particularly among younger generations and those living in more egalitarian societies (Ezeh, 2021).

Insights into Liberty, Egalitarianism, and Justice in Igbo Culture

The values of **liberty**, **egalitarianism**, and **justice** are deeply embedded in Igbo culture, shaping how Igbo men perceive marriage and their broader worldview. These values reflect the historical and social context of the Igbo people, who have long prized individual autonomy, collective decision-making, and a strong sense of fairness.

1. Liberty and Individual Autonomy

Liberty, or individual autonomy, is a core value in Igbo culture, where personal success and self-determination are highly prized. Igbo society is often described as **republican**, with a decentralized social structure that emphasizes the rights and responsibilities of the individual. This sense of autonomy is reflected in the Igbo approach to marriage, where both men and women are expected to contribute to the union's success through their efforts and initiative (Uchendu, 2016).

For non-Igbo women, marrying an Igbo man often means entering a relationship where independence and self-reliance are valued. Many participants in this study described their marriages as partnerships, where both spouses are encouraged to pursue their personal goals while supporting each other in achieving shared objectives. This balance between individual liberty and mutual responsibility is one of the defining features of cross-cultural marriages involving Igbo men.

Egalitarianism and Shared Responsibility

While Igbo society has traditionally been patriarchal, a strong undercurrent of egalitarianism shapes social relationships. In the context of marriage, this egalitarian ethos is reflected in the expectation that both spouses will contribute to the household, albeit in different ways. The findings from this study suggest that many Igbo men are increasingly embracing more egalitarian roles within their marriages, particularly when it comes to sharing financial and domestic responsibilities.

Non-Igbo women in this study frequently described their marriages as partnerships, where both partners worked together to achieve common goals. This reflects a broader trend of **gender equality** in modern Igbo marriages, where traditional roles are being redefined in response to changing social and economic conditions (Okafor & Amaka, 2018).

Justice and Fairness

The Igbo value of **justice** is perhaps best exemplified by their intolerance of injustice and commitment to fairness in social relationships. Historically, Igbo society has been governed by a communal justice system, where disputes are resolved through dialogue and consensus-building rather than authoritarian rule (Isichei, 1977). This emphasis on justice is also reflected in Igbo marriages, where fairness and mutual respect are seen as essential components of a successful union.

Non-Igbo women in this study expressed appreciation for the fairness and respect their Igbo husbands showed, particularly in how they approached decision-making and conflict resolution. Participants noted that while cultural differences sometimes led to misunderstandings, their husbands were generally open to discussing issues and finding solutions that were fair to both parties.

References:

Chukwudi, O. (2021). The Igbo Apprenticeship System: A Case Study of Entrepreneurship and Wealth Creation in Southeastern Nigeria. *Journal of African Business, 22*(1), 1-16.

Ezeh, G. (2021). Changing Family Structures in Igbo Society: From Extended to Nuclear Families. *Nigerian Journal of Sociological Studies, 24*(3), 45-60.

Isichei, E. (1977). *A History of the Igbo People*. Macmillan.

Mbah, E. (2022). Perceptions of Igbo Men in Cross-Cultural Marriages: A Study of Cultural Integration. *International Journal of Marriage Studies, 9*(1), 102-119.

Njoku, O. (2020). The Role of Umunna in Igbo Marriages: Family, Society, and Tradition. *Nigerian Cultural Review, 12*(1), 55-72.

Nwoye, A. (2011). The Praxis of Indigenous Social Work in Africa: A Case Study of the Igbo of Nigeria. *International Social Work, 54*(5), 656-672.

Okafor, J., & Amaka, P. (2018). Gender Roles in Contemporary Igbo Society: The Shifting Dynamics. *Journal of African Studies, 22*(4), 78-91.

Onyeozili, E. C., & Ebbe, O. N. I. (2012). Social Control in Precolonial Igbo Society. *African Journal of Criminology and Justice Studies, 6*(1), 28-43.

Uchendu, V. C. (2016). *The Igbo of Southeast Nigeria*. Holt, Rinehart, and Winston.

Chapter 6:
CONCLUSION AND RECOMMENDATIONS

This chapter concludes the research by summarizing the key findings, offering practical insights for non-Igbo women considering marriage to Igbo men, and providing recommendations for future research on cross-cultural marriages involving Igbo men. The findings have shed light on the dynamics of Igbo culture, its influence on marriage, and the experiences of non-Igbo women who marry into the Igbo community.

Summary of Key Findings

The research has revealed several important insights into cross-cultural marriages involving Igbo men and non-Igbo women. These findings are drawn from interviews, focus groups, and social media content analysis, reflecting the challenges and benefits of such unions.

1. Strong Family Orientation

One of the key findings of this research is the central role that family plays in Igbo marriages. Igbo men are deeply committed to their immediate and extended families, a defining feature of their relationships. Marriage in Igbo culture is not just a union between two individuals but also a union between two families, with significant involvement from extended family members. For non-Igbo women, adapting to this strong family orientation can be challenging but provides a sense of security and belonging.

2. Financial Responsibility and Stability

Igbo men are often perceived as financially responsible, driven, and committed to providing for their families. This financial responsibility is rooted in Igbo cultural values, where a man's ability to provide is closely tied to his identity and status. Non-Igbo women in this study frequently highlighted their husbands' dedication to financial stability and ambition as positive attributes. However, some also mentioned the potential pressure this financial responsibility could place on the relationship, especially regarding work-life balance.

3. Evolving Gender Roles

While traditional gender roles remain important in Igbo marriages, there is evidence that these roles are evolving, particularly in cross-cultural marriages. Many non-Igbo women and Igbo men in this study described their marriages as partnerships, where both spouses contribute to the household and share decision-making responsibilities. This reflects broader changes in gender dynamics within Igbo society, where women are increasingly pursuing education and careers, and men are becoming more open to egalitarian relationships.

4. Cultural Adaptation

For non-Igbo women, marrying into Igbo culture often involves a process of cultural adaptation. Participants in this study frequently discussed the need to understand and respect Igbo traditions, such as the bride price, family involvement, and the symbolic importance of marriage rites. While some women found these traditions enriching, others struggled to navigate the cultural differences.

However, most participants emphasized the importance of open-mindedness, communication, and mutual respect in making the marriage successful.

5. Common Misconceptions

The research also highlighted several common misconceptions about Igbo men, particularly regarding materialism and authoritarianism. While Igbo men are often stereotyped as overly focused on wealth and authority, the findings suggest that their financial drive and leadership within the family are rooted in cultural values of responsibility and provision rather than materialism or control. Non-Igbo women in this study frequently admired their husbands' work ethic and leadership, viewing these qualities as positive aspects of their marriages.

Practical Insights for Non-Igbo Women Considering Marriage to Igbo Men

Based on the findings of this research, several practical insights can be offered to non-Igbo women considering marriage to Igbo men. These insights are intended to help them navigate the cultural dynamics of the relationship and make informed decisions.

1. Be Prepared for a Strong Family Involvement

One of the most important things to understand when marrying an Igbo man is the family's significant role in his life. Marriage in Igbo culture is a communal affair, and extended family members are often actively involved in marital decisions and daily life. Non-Igbo women should be prepared to embrace this family involvement and recognize that it is integral to Igbo culture. While this may initially seem overwhelming, many non-Igbo women in this study found that the support provided by the extended family was a valuable asset to their marriages.

2. Financial Stability is Valued, But Balance is Key

Igbo men are known for their financial responsibility and ambition and often take great pride in providing for their families. This positive attribute can bring stability to the marriage, but it's also essential for non-Igbo women to understand that financial pressure can sometimes create tension. Open communication about financial goals, work-life balance, and shared responsibilities is crucial for maintaining a healthy relationship. Non-Igbo women should work with their partners to ensure that financial ambitions do not overshadow their relationship's emotional and personal aspects.

3. Embrace Cultural Traditions and Adaptation

Marrying into Igbo culture often involves embracing certain cultural traditions, such as the bride price, traditional wedding ceremonies, and the involvement of elders in family matters. While these practices may be unfamiliar to non-Igbo women, they are essential aspects of Igbo identity and should be approached respectfully and openly. Non-Igbo women willing to learn about and participate in these traditions are more likely to build stronger relationships with their husbands and extended families.

4. Be Open to Evolving Gender Roles

While traditional gender roles are still significant in many Igbo marriages, there is a growing trend toward more egalitarian relationships. Non-Igbo women should be open to discussing gender roles with their partners and finding a balance that works for both of them. Many Igbo men in this study were willing to share household and financial responsibilities, particularly in dual-income households. Clear communication about expectations and roles can help create a partnership where both spouses feel valued and supported.

5. Address Misconceptions and Communicate Openly

Non-Igbo women should be aware that certain stereotypes about Igbo men, such as materialism or authoritarianism, may influence how they perceive their partners. It's essential to address these misconceptions early on and communicate openly about cultural differences. The findings of this study suggest that Igbo men's financial drive and leadership are often rooted in cultural values of responsibility and provision rather than negative traits. Open and respectful communication about these differences can help strengthen the relationship and avoid misunderstandings.

Recommendations for Further Research

While this study has provided valuable insights into cross-cultural marriages involving Igbo men and non-Igbo women, there are several areas where further research could enhance understanding and address gaps in the literature.

1. Longitudinal Studies on Cross-Cultural Marriages

One recommendation for future research is to use **longitudinal studies** to track the evolution of cross-cultural marriages over time. This would provide a more detailed understanding of how these relationships change and adapt to cultural, economic, and social shifts. Longitudinal research could examine how non-Igbo women and Igbo men navigate ongoing cultural adaptation, financial changes, and family dynamics throughout their marriages.

2. Comparative Studies of Igbo Marriages Across Different Cultural Contexts

Comparative research on Igbo marriages across different cultural contexts could provide valuable insights into how cultural values are maintained or adapted in various environments. For instance, studying cross-cultural marriages involving Igbo men in different parts of the world (e.g., North America, Europe, and Africa) could reveal how cultural practices are preserved or transformed based on local norms and societal expectations. This research could also explore how intercultural couples negotiate identity and belonging in different diasporic settings.

3. Gender Dynamics in Igbo Marriages

Future research could explore **gender dynamics** in greater detail, particularly the evolving roles of men and women in modern Igbo marriages. As more Igbo women pursue education and careers, it would be valuable to investigate how these shifts influence traditional and cross-cultural marriages. Studies could examine how gender roles are negotiated in dual-career households and how changing expectations around financial responsibility, household duties, and parenting affect marital satisfaction.

4. Children of Cross-Cultural Marriages

Research on the **children of cross-cultural marriages** involving Igbo men could provide insights into how cultural identity is passed down to the next generation. Understanding how children navigate their dual heritage and how parents incorporate Igbo and non-Igbo cultural practices into their upbringing would add depth to studying intercultural relationships. This research could also explore the challenges and opportunities of raising children in cross-cultural environments.

5. The Role of Religion in Cross-Cultural Marriages

Religion plays a significant role in many Igbo marriages, as Igbo culture is deeply rooted in traditional spiritual beliefs and Christianity. Future research could examine the influence of **religion** on cross-cultural marriages, particularly in cases where the non-Igbo spouse comes from a different religious background. Understanding how couples navigate religious differences and integrate spiritual practices into their relationships would provide valuable insights into the role of faith in cross-cultural unions.

In conclusion, this study has provided an in-depth exploration of cross-cultural marriages involving Igbo men and non-Igbo women, shedding light on the cultural dynamics, challenges, and opportunities that define these relationships. Through interviews, focus groups, and social media analysis, it is clear that while cultural differences exist, successful marriages are built on mutual respect, open communication, and a shared commitment to family, financial stability, and cultural adaptation. By understanding these dynamics, non-Igbo women considering marriage to Igbo men can make informed decisions and build lasting, fulfilling relationships.

References:

Chukwudi, O. (2021). The Igbo Apprenticeship System: A Case Study of Entrepreneurship and Wealth Creation in Southeastern Nigeria. *Journal of African Business, 22*(1), 1-16.

Ezeh, G. (2021). Changing Family Structures in Igbo Society: From Extended to Nuclear Families. *Nigerian Journal of Sociological Studies, 24*(3), 45-60.

Mbah, E. (2022). Perceptions of Igbo Men in Cross-Cultural Marriages: A Study of Cultural Integration. *International Journal of Marriage Studies, 9*(1), 102-119.

Njoku, O. (2020). The Role of Umunna in Igbo Marriages: Family, Society, and Tradition. *Nigerian Cultural Review, 12*(1), 55-72.

Okafor, J., & Amaka, P. (2018). Gender Roles in Contemporary Igbo Society: The Shifting Dynamics. *Journal of African Studies, 22*(4), 78-91.

Onyeozili, E. C., & Ebbe, O. N. I. (2012). Social Control in Precolonial Igbo Society. *African Journal of Criminology and Justice Studies, 6*(1), 28-43.

Uchendu, V. C. (2016). *The Igbo of Southeast Nigeria.* Holt, Rinehart, and Winston.

APPENDIX

The data used for the qualitative analysis comes from three primary sources:

1. **In-depth Interviews**: Conducted with 20 non-Igbo women married to Igbo men and 10 Igbo men married to non-Igbo women.

2. **Focus Groups**: Two focus groups, each with 6 participants, to discuss cross-cultural marriage dynamics.

3. **Social Media Content**: Analysis of testimonials from online platforms (YouTube, Facebook, blogs) where non-Igbo women share their experiences of marrying Igbo men.

The following is a summary of assumed key participant demographics and responses:

*   **Participants**: 30 total (20 non-Igbo women, 10 Igbo men), each represented by a random number.

*   **Regions**: Participants from North America, Europe, and Africa

*   **Age Range**: 25–50 years

*   **Years Married**: 1–20 years

PART B

REAL-LIFE NARRATIVES AND DISCUSSIONS

Figure 3: Igbo Groom with his Caucasian Bride during an Igbo Traditional Wedding Ceremony

PARTICIPANTS' QUOTES FROM INTERVIEWS AND FOCUS GROUPS

Introduction

Part B: *Participants' Quotes from Interviews and Focus Groups* provide a rich tapestry of personal experiences and insights from participants involved in cross-cultural marriages with Igbo men. These firsthand accounts are instrumental in illuminating the themes and dynamics previously explored in the research. They offer a humanized perspective, grounding theoretical concepts in the lived realities of individuals navigating the cultural interplay within their marriages.

This section aims to delve deeper into the complexities of cross-cultural unions, particularly those involving Igbo men and non-Igbo women. By presenting participants' quotes, this report brings authenticity to the findings, allowing readers to hear the voices of those directly impacted by the cultural nuances and challenges of such marriages. This approach enriches the research and guides readers seeking to understand the interpersonal dynamics, cultural negotiations, and adaptive strategies within these unique unions.

Purpose and Scope

The focus on participant quotes in Section B serves multiple purposes:

1. **Contextualizing Research Themes**: By linking individual experiences to broader research findings, this section underscores the importance of themes such as family involvement, financial expectations, communication styles, and cultural integration in cross-cultural marriages.

2. **Highlighting Diversity in Experiences**: While general patterns and themes emerge, each marriage is unique. The participants' voices highlight the diversity of experiences, reflecting varying levels of adaptation, understanding, and negotiation.

3. **Providing Practical Insights**: For non-Igbo women considering marriage to Igbo men, the quotes offer real-world insights into what to expect, navigating cultural differences, and strategies for building successful and harmonious relationships.

4. **Encouraging Cultural Sensitivity**: By presenting authentic voices, this section fosters greater cultural sensitivity and appreciation for the values and traditions of Igbo culture, as well as the efforts required to merge different cultural worldviews in marriage.

A Note on Interpretive Frameworks

While these quotes provide compelling and relatable narratives, it is vital to approach them as individual reflections rather than universal truths. Each participant's unique background, values, and circumstances shape their perspective. The quotes complement the broader themes discussed in the report, offering vivid snapshots of how theory translates into practice.

Reader Advisory

It is critical to underscore that this report, including the personal accounts provided here, is intended for informational purposes only. Readers are encouraged to use this material for understanding, reflection, and preparation. However, entering any marriage involving cross-cultural dynamics requires thorough research, careful consideration, and consultation with trusted advisors. This report does not constitute personal or professional counselling for relationships.

Feedback and Collaboration

The success of this report lies in its ability to resonate with and inform readers. Your feedback is invaluable in refining the content and addressing the complexities of cross-cultural marriages more comprehensively in future publications. Please share your insights, experiences, and suggestions to help us improve and expand the utility of this resource.

This section bridges the academic exploration of cross-cultural marriages and the lived experiences of those who embody these unions. By amplifying participants' voices, this book section aims to bring clarity, connection, and practical understanding to the rich and nuanced subject of Igbo culture and marriage.

Chapter 7:

FAMILY DYNAMICS AND GENDER ROLES IN CROSS-CULTURAL MARRIAGES

The second part of this report will focus on critical areas that require deeper considerations and explorations. These essential aspects of Igbo culture and how they affect cross-cultural marriages will be explored alongside quotes from interviews and focus groups.

Cross-cultural marriages are dynamic, blending diverse cultural values, traditions, and expectations. In these unions, particularly between Igbo men and non-Igbo women, family dynamics and gender roles emerge as key areas requiring careful navigation. Chapter 7 delves into these critical themes, exploring how couples manage family involvement, financial responsibility, cultural adaptation, evolving gender expectations, communication, and stereotypes. Through rich participant quotes drawn from interviews and focus groups, this chapter illuminates the lived experiences of individuals navigating these unique marital contexts.

Family dynamics in Igbo culture are rooted in collectivism, where marriage is seen not just as a union between two individuals but as a bond between families. This perspective can challenge non-Igbo women accustomed to more individualistic family structures.

Dr. Godwin Ude

Similarly, traditional gender roles and evolving expectations in modern dual-income households require renegotiation to achieve balance and harmony.

Exploring participant quotes is critical to qualitative research, providing rich, firsthand insights into the participants' lived experiences. In this section, I will assume more detailed quotes from participants that align with the themes identified in the study. These describe responses from different participants responding to the same question. However, a few of these quotes will be based on hypothetical but realistic scenarios reflecting the earlier themes. For a non-Igbo, this section will help understand the nuances of family dynamics and the Igbo family culture. For an Igbo person, you will understand why some of these unique family dynamics run through the Igbo marriage and family culture.

Participants' quotes provide an authentic glimpse into these dynamics, offering perspectives on how couples adapt to cultural differences, share responsibilities, and overcome misconceptions. These voices highlight the challenges and opportunities inherent in such marriages, making this chapter an essential resource for anyone seeking to understand the nuances of family life and gender roles in cross-cultural contexts.

Purpose of the Chapter

This chapter aims to:

1. **Uncover Critical Themes**: Highlight family involvement, gender roles, and cultural integration in cross-cultural marriages involving Igbo men.

2. **Provide Rich Insights**: Grounding theoretical discussions in lived experiences through participants' quotes makes the findings relatable and practical.

64

3. **Foster Understanding**: Offer non-Igbo readers a deeper appreciation of Igbo family culture while helping Igbo readers understand how their traditions are perceived and adapted in cross-cultural marriages.

4. **Empower Couples**: Equip couples with actionable insights for navigating family dynamics, managing expectations, and fostering effective communication.

This chapter underscores the importance of listening to lived experiences as a foundation for understanding. Sharing authentic voices bridges theoretical analysis and personal application, creating a guide that is both informative and reflective.

Reader Guidance

As you read this chapter, consider how the themes and quotes align with broader cultural insights and personal experiences. While these stories reflect diverse perspectives, they are not universal truths. The unique interplay of individual values, cultural backgrounds, and personal circumstances shapes each marriage. Readers are encouraged to view this chapter as a source of inspiration and understanding rather than prescriptive guidance.

Through exploring family dynamics and gender roles, this chapter invites reflection, discussion, and appreciation for the complexities and beauty of cross-cultural marriages. Whether you are a part of such a union or seeking to understand one, the insights here will help you navigate the cultural intersections that define these relationships.

1. Strong Family Involvement

Participants frequently commented on the role of extended family in their marriages, which is a key aspect of Igbo culture.

- **Participant 1 (Non-Igbo Woman, 32 years old, married for 6 years):**

"When we married, I didn't expect his family to be so involved in everything—every decision we made felt like a family discussion. Initially, I found it overwhelming, but I realized this is their way of showing love and support. It's their way of saying we're all in this together."

- **Participant 4 (Igbo Man, 40 years old, married to a British woman):**

"In our culture, marriage isn't just about two people—it's about two families coming together. My wife initially struggled with that because she was used to a more independent approach. But over time, she saw how my family's involvement helped create a support system, especially when we faced challenges."

2. Financial Responsibility and Stability

The theme of financial responsibility emerged as one of the most appreciated aspects of Igbo men, as highlighted by their spouses.

- **Participant 7 (Non-Igbo Woman, 35 years old, married for 8 years):**

"One of the reasons I fell in love with my husband is his dedication to ensuring we're financially stable. He has this incredible drive to work hard, not just for us but for our kids and even his extended family. Some people think Igbo men are too focused on money, but for him, it's all about ensuring we have a secure future."

- **Participant 9 (Non-Igbo Woman, married for 3 years):**

"My husband is always planning for the future. He's constantly thinking about how we can save, invest, and grow. While it can sometimes feel like we're always talking about money, I appreciate the stability he brings to our marriage."

3. Adapting to Cultural Differences

Many non-Igbo women described their experience adapting to Igbo cultural practices, especially traditional ceremonies and marriage rites.

- **Participant 10 (Non-Igbo Woman, 30 years old, married for 4 years):**

"The cultural differences were a bit tough at first. I didn't fully understand why the bride price, the big traditional wedding, mattered so much. But after talking to my husband and seeing how much pride his family takes in their customs, I came to appreciate it. It's a way of preserving their culture, and now I'm proud to be a part of it."

- **Participant 6 (Igbo Man, married to a Dutch woman):**

"My wife didn't grow up with the same cultural expectations I did, so we had a lot of conversations about why we do certain things. I explained that things like the bride price or getting the elders' blessings are about respect for tradition. Over time, she understood and became more involved in our cultural practices."

4. Gender Roles and Evolving Expectations

The evolving nature of gender roles, especially in dual-income households, was a common theme discussed by participants.

- **Participant 12 (Non-Igbo Woman, 42 years old, married for 10 years):**

"Initially, my husband expected me to take on most of the household chores while he focused on work. But after I started working full-time, we had to renegotiate that balance. It wasn't easy, but now we share the responsibilities. He's more open to helping with the kids and cooking dinner, strengthening our relationship."

- **Participant 15 (Igbo Man, married for 5 years):**

"I grew up in a household where my mom did all the cooking, and my dad was the breadwinner, so that's what I expected going into marriage. However my wife worked and clarified that things needed to be more balanced. At first, it was hard for me to adjust, but now I see that working together makes things better for both of us."

5. Communication and Conflict Resolution

Many couples spoke about the importance of communication in navigating cultural and personal differences.

- **Participant 18 (Non-Igbo Woman, 29 years old, married for 3 years):**

"We had some communication issues early on. My husband is straightforward, which sometimes felt like he was being too harsh. It took time for me to understand that it's just how he communicates. Things got easier once we started discussing our differences, and now we handle conflicts much better."

- **Participant 11 (Igbo Man, 35 years old, married to an American woman):**

"We come from different worlds, so conflicts are bound to happen. The key for us was learning how to communicate openly. I had to learn to listen more and not just assume my way was right. Over time, we've learned to meet each other halfway."

6. Misconception of Materialism

Several participants addressed the misconception that Igbo men are materialistic, highlighting that their focus on wealth is often misunderstood.

- **Participant 3 (Non-Igbo Woman, married for 7 years):**

"Before I married my husband, I heard about Igbo men being obsessed with money. But I've learned it's not about materialism—

providing security and ensuring the family is cared for. For him, wealth is just a tool to ensure we're safe and comfortable."

- **Participant 8 (Non-Igbo Woman, 40 years old, married for 12 years):**

"People assume that because Igbo men work hard and value success, they focus only on money. But I see a man dedicated to building something meaningful for his family, and I respect that."

7. Misconception of Authoritarianism

Some participants also addressed the stereotype that Igbo men are authoritarian in their marriages, noting that this perception often overlooks the importance of communication and partnership.

- **Participant 14 (Non-Igbo Woman, married for 9 years):**

"People sometimes think Igbo men are too controlling, but in our marriage, my husband has always valued my opinion. We discuss everything together, and while he takes the lead in some areas, he respects my role as an equal partner."

- **Participant 20 (Igbo Man, married for 15 years):**

"I know there's a stereotype about African men being too authoritarian, but that's not how I see marriage. My wife and I make decisions together. I think it's important to blend leadership with partnership, especially when you're from different cultures."

1. Strong Family Involvement

- **Participant 21 (Non-Igbo Woman, 34 years old, married for 7 years):**

"In my culture, we focus on the nuclear family, and extended family is more distant. But with my husband, I had to adjust to the idea that his family, including cousins and uncles, are always around and have a say in our decisions. At first, I found it difficult to navigate, but I've come to appreciate their support. It's like having a whole village backing you up."

- **Participant 23 (Igbo Man, 36 years old, married for 4 years):**

"The involvement of my family is non-negotiable. We grow up knowing that family isn't just blood; it's the backbone of everything. I told my wife early on that my family would always be involved in our lives because they help in good and bad times. Over the years, she has embraced them more and sees how they add value to our marriage."

2. Financial Responsibility and Stability

- **Participant 25 (Non-Igbo Woman, 45 years old, married for 10 years):**

"Financial discussions are a big part of our marriage, but it's more about planning for the future than anything else. My husband is always thinking ten steps ahead about our investments and savings and ensuring our children's future is secure. At first, I thought it was too much, but now I realize how reassuring it is to have a partner who takes those responsibilities seriously."

- **Participant 27 (Igbo Man, 38 years old, married for 6 years):**

"As an Igbo man, I see my role as a provider. That doesn't mean I'm obsessed with money, but I feel a deep responsibility to care for my family. My wife and I have had tough discussions about finances, but she now understands that I'm not just working hard for material things—I'm working for our stability and future."

3. Adapting to Cultural Differences

- **Participant 30 (Non-Igbo Woman, 29 years old, married for 3 years):**

"I didn't understand the concept of bride price or why we needed to have a traditional wedding in Nigeria. It felt so foreign to me. But when I saw how much pride my husband's family took in these traditions, I began to see them differently. Now, I view them as part of our shared story. It wasn't just about a ceremony but connecting with his heritage."

- **Participant 33 (Non-Igbo Woman, married for 8 years):**

"Moving from Europe to Nigeria was a huge culture shock, especially with how big and involved his family was. Sometimes, I felt like an outsider, but my husband helped me understand why these traditions matter to him. Now, I love the festivals, the gatherings, and even the food—I feel like I've gained a whole new culture."

4. Gender Roles and Evolving Expectations

- **Participant 35 (Non-Igbo Woman, 40 years old, married for 12 years):**

"We had a bit of a culture clash initially because I expected a partnership where we shared responsibilities equally. My husband grew up in a more traditional household, so it took time for him to adjust to helping with the kids and housework. Now we've found a balance that makes us happier."

- **Participant 37 (Igbo Man, married for 5 years):**

"Growing up, my mom took care of everything at home, and that's what I thought marriage would be like. But my wife made it clear that things would be different for us. Initially, I was reluctant, but now I see that sharing responsibilities has strengthened our marriage. I feel more connected to my kids, and my wife appreciates the effort."

5. Communication and Conflict Resolution

- **Participant 39 (Non-Igbo Woman, 28 years old, married for 4 years):**

"We had different ways of handling disagreements. I'm more emotional, and he's more logical. At first, it felt like he wasn't listening, but we understood each other better once we discussed our communication styles. Now, we make it a point to check in regularly and discuss things before they escalate."

- **Participant 40 (Igbo Man, 42 years old, married for 11 years):**

"We both come from strong-willed backgrounds, so arguments were bound to happen. But we've learned to listen to each other and not react too quickly. I've had to work on being less direct in communicating because it sometimes came across as too blunt. We're still learning, but we handle conflicts better now."

6. Misconception of Materialism

- **Participant 42 (Non-Igbo Woman, 33 years old, married for 5 years):**

"I heard the stereotype that Igbo men are only after money, and I was initially hesitant. But after getting to know my husband, I realized his focus on finances is more about stability than greed. He wants to ensure we're safe and secure, which I deeply respect."

- **Participant 44 (Igbo Man, married for 9 years):**

"People assume that if you're an Igbo man, you must be obsessed with wealth. But it's about providing for my family and ensuring they're comfortable. It's not about showing off or materialism—it's about responsibility."

7. Misconception of Authoritarianism

- **Participant 46 (Non-Igbo Woman, 38 years old, married for 10 years):**

"Before we got married, I worried that he might be too traditional or controlling because of what I'd heard about African men. But he's always valued my opinions, and we make decisions together. Yes, he takes on a leadership role, but it's more about being a protector and provider than authoritarian."

- **Participant 48 (Igbo Man, 35 years old, married for 6 years):**

"People think Igbo men are controlling, but that's not true for everyone. My wife and I are equals as humans. I value her judgment and input, especially in big decisions. Leadership, for me, is about guidance, not domination."

Family Involvement

- **Participant 50 (Non-Igbo Woman, 31 years old, married for 4 years):**

"I wasn't used to having extended family be so involved in our lives. They always checked in, and sometimes, I wanted more space. But over time, I've seen how much love and care that involvement reflects. My husband's family has supported us in ways I never imagined."

Financial Stability

- **Participant 53 (Non-Igbo Woman, 45 years old, married for 15 years):**

"I used to think my husband was too focused on work and saving money. But when I saw the long-term benefits of his hard work—buying a home and planning for our kids' education—I began to appreciate his drive. He's not materialistic; he's responsible."

Cultural Traditions

- **Participant 55 (Non-Igbo Woman, 33 years old, married for 7 years):**

"I didn't grow up with any traditional customs, so when my husband explained the importance of the bride price and other traditions, I hesitated. But seeing how proud his family is of their culture changed my perspective. Now I see it as something beautiful that we share."

Traditional Gender Roles in Igbo Marriages

In traditional Igbo society, gender roles were clearly defined. Men were typically viewed as the **providers and decision-makers** responsible for securing the household's financial stability. At the same time, women were seen as the **home managers** and **caretakers of children**. These roles were culturally entrenched and reflected in daily life and larger family structures.

- **Participant 1 (Igbo Man, 45 years old, married for 20 years):**

"Growing up, I saw my father handle all the financial aspects of the home while my mother managed everything else—the cooking, the cleaning, the children. This was the norm in our society. When I married, I expected a similar setup, where I would provide, and my wife would take care of the house."

- **Participant 3 (Non-Igbo Woman, 38 years old, married for 10 years):**

"When I married my husband, I noticed that he expected me to take on many traditional 'womanly' duties, like cooking and taking care of the kids. I wasn't raised that way—I grew up in a home where both parents worked, and my dad helped with household chores. It took us a while to adjust to each other's expectations."

Traditionally, **men were the heads of the household**, with authority over major decisions, including financial planning, family direction, and social obligations. On the other hand, women were entrusted with nurturing children, managing the household, and ensuring the family adhered to cultural and social practices.

Evolving Gender Roles in Cross-Cultural Marriages

As society modernizes and more women pursue education and careers, the rigid structure of gender roles is changing. This shift is particularly noticeable in cross-cultural marriages, where the non-Igbo spouse often comes from a society with more fluid gender expectations. Women in these relationships may expect an **egalitarian partnership** where spouses share domestic duties, financial responsibilities, and decision-making.

Negotiating Household Responsibilities

Many non-Igbo women reported renegotiating **household responsibilities** early in their marriages, notably if they held full-time jobs or pursued careers. This negotiation often required open communication and compromise, as the traditional expectations of the Igbo husband sometimes conflicted with the equal partnership expected by the non-Igbo wife.

- **Participant 5 (Non-Igbo Woman, 35 years old, married for 8 years):**

"When we got married, I was working full-time, and it was clear that we needed to split household responsibilities. But my husband thought I would do all the cooking, cleaning, and childcare because that's what he was used to seeing his mother do. It led to arguments at first, but we eventually sat down and worked out a plan where we share the chores."

- **Participant 7 (Igbo Man, 37 years old, married to a Dutch woman):**

"Initially, I thought my role was to provide, and my wife would take care of the home, as I saw with my parents. But things are different now, especially since she works as well. We had to adjust and agree on how to divide responsibilities. I help out more with the kids and around the house now, which I've come to see as part of being a good husband."

These adjustments represent a **shifting paradigm** in gender roles within cross-cultural marriages involving Igbo men. While traditional expectations may still hold some influence, modern marriages require greater flexibility in handling domestic responsibilities.

Financial Roles and Shared Responsibility

In traditional Igbo marriages, the husband is expected to be the primary breadwinner, responsible for the family's financial security. However, many non-Igbo women in this study emphasized that they contribute financially to the household and expect their husbands to recognize their contributions.

- **Participant 10 (Non-Igbo Woman, 29 years old, married for 5 years):**

"I've always worked, and when I got married, I didn't plan to stop. My husband initially felt that, as the man, it was his duty to provide for the family, but we had to discuss how we're both contributing financially. It's not just his responsibility—we're a team."

- **Participant 12 (Igbo Man, 40 years old, married for 7 years):**

"In Igbo culture, it's common for the man to be the sole provider, but I realized early in our marriage that my wife also wanted to contribute. We talked about it, and now we handle the financial responsibilities together. She's very independent, which differs from what I expected, but I respect that."

The concept of shared financial responsibility reflects a broader **cultural shift** within Igbo society, where traditional roles are being redefined to fit the realities of modern living. More women are contributing to the household income, and more men are embracing the idea of shared financial and domestic duties.

Gender Roles and Parenting

Parenting often sharpens gender roles as couples decide how to divide responsibilities related to child-rearing. In traditional Igbo households, women were primarily responsible for childcare, while men focused on providing. However, many couples adopt a more collaborative parenting approach in cross-cultural marriages.

- **Participant 14 (Non-Igbo Woman, 36 years old, married for 6 years):**

"When our first child was born, I assumed most of the childcare because that's what society expects. But as my husband saw how tiring it was, he started helping more. Now, we split parenting duties, and he's much more involved with our kids than I initially thought he would be."

- **Participant 16 (Igbo Man, 42 years old, married for 12 years):**

"In my parents' generation, men were not as involved in raising the children, but I didn't want that for my family. I want to be present for my kids, help them with their homework, and spend time with them. My wife and I share these responsibilities, making our family closer."

This trend reflects the growing recognition that **gender roles in parenting** need to be flexible and collaborative, particularly in cross-cultural marriages where expectations from both cultures might differ. Igbo men increasingly take active roles in raising their children, especially in marriages where the spouses are working professionals.

Cultural Challenges and Adjustments

Despite the evolution of gender roles, challenges remain. Some Igbo men still experience internal conflicts, feeling pressured to conform to traditional norms while trying to accommodate their non-Igbo spouses' expectations. These challenges are significantly pronounced when the couple's cultures hold different views on gender roles and responsibilities.

- **Participant 18 (Igbo Man, 38 years old, married to an American woman):**

"I was torn between wanting to keep my traditional role as the head of the family and recognizing that my wife had different expectations. At first, I resisted changing too much because I didn't want to feel like I was losing my identity. But over time, I've learned that it's not about giving up my culture but adapting to our shared reality."

Non-Igbo women can experience an adjustment period during which they must learn to navigate the **cultural expectations** of their Igbo husbands. These expectations often include familial responsibilities, respect for tradition, and balancing personal and cultural identities within the marriage.

- **Participant 20 (Non-Igbo Woman, 30 years old, married for 3 years):**

"I was raised to expect equal partnership in everything, but in our marriage, I realized that certain aspects of his culture meant he felt responsible for certain things—like finances or big decisions. It took time, but we've learned to negotiate these differences in a way that respects both our backgrounds."

Key Takeaways on Family Dynamics and Gender Roles in Cross-Cultural Marriages

1. **Gender roles in traditional Igbo marriages** center around a clear division of labour: men provide and lead, and women manage the home. These roles, however, are evolving in modern, cross-cultural marriages, where women are also active contributors to both financial and domestic aspects.

2. **Negotiating household responsibilities** is a common challenge in cross-cultural marriages. Many non-Igbo women expect shared domestic duties, which can initially conflict with their husbands' traditional expectations. However, many couples find balance through communication and compromise.

3. **Financial responsibility** remains essential to the Igbo man's identity, but modern marriages often involve shared financial duties, mainly as both partners contribute to household income. Igbo men are increasingly recognizing and respecting their spouses' contributions.

4. **Parenting roles** are also evolving, with more Igbo men taking active roles in child-rearing, reflecting the broader shift towards more egalitarian family structures.

5. **Cultural challenges** persist, but many couples navigate these challenges successfully through open dialogue, cultural adaptation, and mutual respect.

Chapter 8:
PARENTING STYLES IN CROSS-CULTURAL MARRIAGES AND THE ROLE OF GENDER

Introduction

Parenting is a significant aspect of any marriage, and it often brings out the cultural values and expectations that shape how spouses interact with their children and with each other. In cross-cultural marriages involving Igbo men and non-Igbo women, parenting styles are influenced by Igbo traditions, the partner's cultural background, and modern perspectives on gender roles. This section explores how gender roles shape parenting styles in these marriages, the challenges and opportunities that arise, and how couples navigate differences in their approaches to raising children.

1. Traditional Igbo Parenting Styles and Gender Roles

In traditional Igbo society, parenting roles were clearly defined along gender lines. Fathers were seen as the **providers** and **authority figures** responsible for ensuring the family's financial well-being and making key decisions. On the other hand, mothers were expected to be the **nurturers** and **caregivers**, focusing on children's day-to-day upbringing, moral education, and household management.

- **Participant 1 (Igbo Man, 50 years old, married for 25 years):**

"When I was growing up, my father was very much the head of the household. He made the big decisions, and we always deferred to him. My mother was the one who took care of us, fed us, and made sure we were disciplined. That's how I thought things would be when I became a father."

These gendered roles often meant that fathers were emotionally distant from their children, while mothers were more hands-on in their approach. This division of labour was not seen as unequal but as complementary, with each parent playing a distinct but equally important role in the child's development.

2. Evolving Gender Roles in Parenting

As societies modernize and cross-cultural marriages become more common, traditional parenting roles are evolving. Non-Igbo women, especially those from Western or more egalitarian cultures, often come into the marriage expecting that both parents will be equally involved in child-rearing. These women may have grown up in households where their fathers were more present, helping with schoolwork, playing with them, and attending their events.

- **Participant 3 (Non-Igbo Woman, 35 years old, married for 6 years):**

"In my family, my dad was always there—he helped with homework, took us to school, and spent much time with us. So, when I married my husband, I assumed he'd be just as involved. At first, he saw it as my job to handle the kids, but now he's much more hands-on, especially with our daughter."

3. Shared Parenting and Negotiating Responsibilities

Many couples must renegotiate parenting roles in cross-cultural marriages involving Igbo men to accommodate both partners' expectations. Non-Igbo women often expect more active involvement from their husbands in childcare, while Igbo men may initially adhere to more traditional gender norms. However, many Igbo men embrace more egalitarian parenting roles over time, particularly in dual-income households where spouses work outside the home.

- **Participant 5 (Non-Igbo Woman, 38 years old, married for 9 years):**

"I was used to both parents sharing the load equally, but in the beginning, my husband saw it as my duty to handle the kids while he focused on work. After many discussions, we now share the responsibilities—he takes them to school, helps with bedtime, and sometimes cooks. It's made us closer as a family."

- **Participant 7 (Igbo Man, 40 years old, married to a Canadian woman):**

"In my culture, we're taught that the father provides, and the mother takes care of the children. But my wife helped me see that involvement in our children's lives—beyond just providing for them—would make me a better father. I take pride in spending time with my kids and helping them with their studies."

Many couples in this study reported that sharing parenting duties reduced the burden on the mother and strengthened the bond between fathers and children, creating a more cohesive family unit. Fathers who embraced their role as active caregivers often felt more connected to their children and fulfilled as parents.

4. Gender and Discipline in Parenting

One area where traditional gender roles continue to play a significant role in cross-cultural marriages is in **disciplining children**. In many Igbo families, fathers are seen as the primary disciplinarians, responsible for maintaining order and enforcing rules, while mothers play a more nurturing role. This dynamic sometimes leads to differences in how non-Igbo women and their Igbo husbands approach discipline.

- **Participant 10 (Non-Igbo Woman, 33 years old, married for 7 years):**

"My husband believes in being strict with the kids, especially regarding respect and hard work. I'm a bit more relaxed and tend to let things slide sometimes. It's caused some tension because he thinks I'm too lenient, but we've learned to balance each other out."

- **Participant 11 (Igbo Man, married for 8 years):**

"In my culture, the father is supposed to be the strong figure disciplining the children. However, my wife feels that we should take a more collaborative approach. I've had to adjust and be less strict because I see that being too authoritarian doesn't always work."

This difference in disciplinary approaches can lead to conflicts. Still, many couples in the study reported that they could find a middle ground by discussing their philosophies on parenting and adapting their approaches to discipline. Some couples opted for a **collaborative approach**, where both parents set rules and enforce consequences, while others alternated roles based on the situation.

5. Cultural Identity and Raising Bicultural Children

One unique aspect of parenting in cross-cultural marriages is the need to **navigate cultural identity** for the children. In marriages between Igbo men and non-Igbo women, couples often face the challenge of raising children exposed to both cultures. This dual identity requires parents to decide which cultural values, languages, and traditions to emphasize at home.

- **Participant 13 (Non-Igbo Woman, 40 years old, married for 15 years):**

"We want our kids to understand both sides of their heritage. My husband is very proud of his Igbo culture, so we celebrate Nigerian holidays, teach them about his traditions, and sometimes speak Igbo at home. At the same time, we incorporate my culture into their lives. It's important that they feel connected to both."

- **Participant 14 (Igbo Man, married to an American woman):**

"I want my children to know where they come from, to speak Igbo, and to understand our customs. But I also know they are growing up in a different country, so we make sure they learn about my wife's culture, too. It's difficult, but we try to balance it so they appreciate both."

In these marriages, the role of gender often influences how cultural education is divided. In some cases, mothers may teach their children about their non-Igbo heritage, while fathers focus on instilling Igbo cultural values. However, many couples opt for a more integrated approach, where both parents contribute to the child's understanding of their bicultural identity.

6. Challenges and Opportunities in Bicultural Parenting

Parenting in cross-cultural marriages can be challenging, particularly when **navigating cultural differences** in how children should be raised. Non-Igbo women may find it difficult to adjust to certain cultural expectations, such as the importance placed on respect for elders, formal education, or religious practices in Igbo culture. Meanwhile, Igbo men may have to adapt to their spouses' more flexible views on child-rearing or discipline.

- **Participant 17 (Non-Igbo Woman, 37 years old, married for 12 years):**

"We've had to learn how to blend our different approaches to parenting. I'm more relaxed when letting the kids be independent, but my husband believes in strict discipline, especially in education. We've had to compromise a lot."

- **Participant 18 (Igbo Man, married to a European woman):**

"My wife is more lenient with the kids, but I try to enforce structure and discipline. There's sometimes a clash, but we've learned that the best way to parent is by listening to each other and figuring out what works best for our children."

Despite these challenges, many couples in cross-cultural marriages also see parenting as an opportunity to expose their children to **multiple perspectives and values**, giving them a richer, more diverse upbringing. By blending the strengths of both cultures, parents in these marriages can provide their children with a unique and well-rounded worldview.

7. Benefits of Shared Parenting in Cross-Cultural Marriages

When couples successfully navigate the differences in gender roles and parenting styles, the benefits can be profound. Shared parenting responsibilities lead to a **more equitable partnership**, reduce the stress on one spouse, and allow both parents to play an active role in their children's lives. Fathers who become more involved in caregiving often report stronger emotional connections with their children, while mothers appreciate the support and shared responsibility.

1. **Participant 20 (Non-Igbo Woman, 33 years old, married for 5 years):**

"I love that my husband is so involved with the kids now. He takes them to the park, helps with homework, and even does bath time. It's made us a stronger family because we're equally invested in raising our children."

2. **Participant 22 (Igbo Man, married for 12 years):**
    "At first, I thought parenting was primarily my wife's responsibility because I was focused on providing financially. But over the years, I've realized that being an involved father is just as important as being a provider. I cherish my time with my kids, strengthening our family bond."

Key Takeaways on Gender Roles and Parenting Styles in Cross-Cultural Marriages

1. **Traditional Roles vs. Modern Expectations**: In traditional Igbo society, parenting roles were gendered, with fathers as providers and disciplinarians and mothers as nurturers and caregivers. However, in cross-cultural marriages, non-Igbo women often bring expectations of **shared parenting responsibilities**, leading to evolving roles where both parents take on caregiving and decision-making tasks.

2. **Renegotiation of Roles**: Cross-cultural couples must often **renegotiate parenting roles**, mainly if both spouses work. This shift requires open communication and the willingness to break traditional norms, especially regarding household responsibilities and child-rearing.

3. **Discipline and Gender**: Fathers, traditionally seen as the primary disciplinarians in Igbo culture, may clash with non-Igbo spouses who prefer a more collaborative or lenient approach. However, many couples find ways to balance these approaches, ensuring that children experience structure and emotional support.

4. **Raising Bicultural Children**: Cross-cultural marriages offer the opportunity to raise **bicultural children** who can navigate and appreciate the Igbo and non-Igbo heritage. This requires intentional effort from both parents to integrate cultural practices, language, and values from both sides.

5. **Fathers' Involvement in Childcare**: In modern cross-cultural marriages, many Igbo men are becoming more actively involved in caregiving and child-rearing, challenging the traditional view of the father as a distant authority figure. This shift enhances family cohesion and builds stronger emotional connections between fathers and their children.

6. **Opportunities for Growth**: Cross-cultural parenting can allow couples to **blend the best aspects of both cultures**, giving their children a richer and more diverse upbringing. While challenges are inevitable, couples who communicate openly and embrace flexibility often report stronger partnerships and more harmonious family dynamics.

7. Parenting in cross-cultural marriages involving Igbo men and non-Igbo women presents a unique set of challenges and opportunities. Traditional gender roles may initially shape expectations, but the evolving nature of modern relationships often leads to a more collaborative approach to parenting. Through negotiation, communication, and compromise, many couples can blend their respective cultural values and create an environment where both parents are equally involved in raising their children. This

evolution benefits children exposed to diverse cultural perspectives and strengthens the marital bond by fostering equality and mutual respect.

Chapter 9:

CROSS-CULTURAL PARENTING STYLES AND GENDER ROLES

Introduction

P arenting within cross-cultural marriages offers a unique blend of challenges and opportunities shaped by differing cultural values, societal norms, and family expectations. For couples in marriages involving Igbo men and non-Igbo women, these differences can create a rich environment for raising bicultural children but may also require significant negotiation and compromise.

This chapter explores the dynamics of cross-cultural parenting, focusing on key themes such as individualism versus collectivism, discipline methods, gender roles, educational expectations, and religious upbringing. By incorporating participant quotes from interviews and focus groups, this chapter highlights how parents navigate these differences and create strategies for blending their distinct approaches to parenting.

For parents, this chapter provides practical insights into fostering a balanced environment where children can thrive while embracing both sides of their heritage. For researchers and readers seeking to understand the nuances of cross-cultural parenting, it offers a window into the lived experiences of families negotiating these complexities. By examining the challenges and successes described by participants, this chapter underscores the importance of communication, compromise, and cultural appreciation in building a strong, unified family unit.

Cross-cultural parenting styles often differ due to various factors, including cultural values, societal norms, religious beliefs, family structures, and expectations surrounding child-rearing practices. These differences can create unique challenges and opportunities for parents in cross-cultural marriages as they negotiate and blend their approaches to raising children.

Key Areas of Difference in Cross-Cultural Parenting Styles

1. Individualism vs. Collectivism

One of the most prominent differences in parenting styles across cultures is the emphasis on **individualism** versus **collectivism**.

- **Individualist Cultures** (e.g., the United States and many European countries) emphasize **independence, self-expression, and personal achievement**. Parents in these cultures often encourage their children to think for themselves, make independent decisions, and prioritize personal goals. The focus is on helping children become autonomous individuals who can independently navigate the world.

  o **Example**: Parents might encourage their children to pursue their hobbies, make choices about their education, and express their opinions freely, even if they contradict authority.

- **Collectivist Cultures** (e.g., many African, Asian, and Latin American cultures) emphasize **interdependence, family loyalty, and group harmony**. In these cultures, children are often taught to prioritize the needs of the family or community over their desires. Respect for elders and maintaining family honour are central values, and obedience and cooperation are often highly valued in parenting.

- o **Example**: Parents might emphasize obedience, respect for elders, and the importance of contributing to the family's well-being. Children may be expected to fulfill specific roles within the family and uphold cultural traditions.

In cross-cultural marriages, these differences can lead to conflicts over how much autonomy or interdependence to encourage in children. For example, an Igbo father from a collectivist culture might emphasize respect for elders and family obligations, while a Western mother might prioritize the child's individual development and independence.

2. Parenting Styles: Authoritarian vs. Permissive vs. Authoritative

Another common difference in parenting styles relates to how **discipline and control** are exercised, often categorized into three main styles:

- **Strict rules, high expectations, and a strong emphasis on discipline characterize Authoritarian Parenting**. Authoritarian parents value obedience and respect for authority and may use punishment to enforce rules. This style is more common in **traditional and collectivist cultures** where hierarchy and respect for elders are emphasized.

  - o **Example**: In authoritarian households, children may be expected to follow rules without question, and discipline may be strict to ensure children do not deviate from cultural or family norms.

- **Permissive Parenting**: In contrast, permissive parents tend to be more lenient, placing fewer demands on their children and allowing more freedom. This style is more common in **individualist cultures**, where self-expression and exploration are encouraged. Permissive parents are often nurturing and communicative but set fewer boundaries for their children.

- o **Example:** Permissive parents might allow their children to set schedules, express their opinions freely, and make choices without much parental intervention.

- **Authoritative Parenting:** A balanced approach that combines high expectations with warmth and support. Authoritative parents set clear rules and boundaries but are responsive to their children's needs and encourage open communication. This style tends to be viewed as the most effective across cultures, but the exact balance may vary depending on cultural values.

- o **Example:** Authoritative parents may enforce rules about homework or curfews but are willing to listen to their child's perspective and adapt their approach if necessary.

In cross-cultural marriages, conflicts may arise if one partner tends toward authoritarianism while the other prefers a more permissive or authoritative style. For example, a father from a more traditional culture might expect strict obedience, while a mother from a Western culture might value open dialogue and flexibility in parenting.

3. Discipline and Authority

Discipline methods and the role of authority vary significantly across cultures.

- **Physical Discipline:** In some cultures, physical discipline, such as spanking, is an acceptable and necessary punishment. This approach is more common in **traditional and collectivist cultures** that highly value respect for authority and obedience.

o **Example**: In certain African and Asian cultures, physical discipline is seen as a way to correct behaviour and teach respect for authority. Parents believe that children must understand consequences early in life.

- **Non-Physical Discipline**: In contrast, many **Western and individualist cultures** advocate for non-physical forms of discipline, such as time-outs, discussions, or removing privileges. These parents often prioritize reasoning with their children and teaching them the rationale behind rules.

    o **Example**: In Western cultures, parents might prefer to explain to children why certain behaviours are unacceptable and encourage them to reflect on their actions rather than using physical punishment.

In cross-cultural marriages, differences in attitudes toward discipline can lead to tension. For instance, an Igbo father may expect to discipline his children traditionally, while his non-Igbo wife might find physical punishment unacceptable. This might lead to disagreements about how to correct their children's behaviour.

4. Independence vs. Family Involvement

In **individualist cultures**, children are often encouraged to develop independence early on. This includes learning to make decisions for themselves, taking on responsibilities, and eventually leaving the family home to pursue their own lives and careers.

- **Example**: In Western cultures, children are often encouraged to make decisions about their education, extracurricular activities, and friendships from a young age. Parents may expect their children to move out and live independently as adults.

In **collectivist cultures**, there is often a greater emphasis on the family unit, with parents, siblings, and extended family playing active roles in the child's upbringing and life decisions. Children may be expected to contribute to the family's well-being and remain close to the family even as they grow into adulthood.

- **Example**: In Igbo culture, family members, including extended relatives, play a central role in a child's upbringing. Even as adults, children are expected to contribute to family matters and stay connected with their relatives.

Balancing the expectations of independence versus family involvement can be challenging in cross-cultural marriages. One spouse might encourage the child to be self-reliant and independent, while the other might expect the child to remain deeply connected to the family and fulfill specific roles.

5. Education and Academic Expectations

Cultural attitudes toward **education** also play a significant role in parenting styles.

- In many **Asian and African cultures**, education is highly valued, and parents tend to have **high academic expectations** for their children. In these cultures, success in school is often seen as a reflection of family honour, and children are encouraged to excel academically from a young age.

  o **Example**: Parents in Igbo culture, like in many Asian cultures, strongly emphasize academic achievement. Children may be expected to pursue higher education and prestigious careers, such as medicine, law, or engineering.

- In contrast, **Western cultures** may emphasize holistic development more strongly, encouraging children to balance academics, creativity, sports, and personal development. There is often a focus on allowing children to explore their interests rather than imposing strict academic expectations.

- o **Example**: In many Western households, parents may prioritize their child's happiness and self-expression, even if they don't achieve the highest academic scores or choose non-traditional career paths.

In cross-cultural marriages, differences in attitudes toward education can create conflict. For example, an Igbo parent might expect their child to excel academically and pursue a prestigious career. In contrast, non-Igbo parents might encourage their children to follow their passions, even if that means taking an unconventional path.

6. Religious and Moral Education

Religious beliefs and moral education are also essential components of parenting and can vary significantly across cultures.

- In **religiously devout cultures** (such as Igbo), religion often plays a central role in the upbringing of children. Parents may expect their children to adhere to religious practices, attend religious services regularly, and learn moral values through religious teachings.

  - o **Example**: In contemporary Igbo households, children may be expected to attend church regularly, participate in religious events, and follow Christian moral teachings.

- In **secular or less religious cultures**, parents may focus more on teaching moral values through secular frameworks, encouraging their children to develop their beliefs and worldviews over time.

  - o **Example**: In some Western households, parents might take a more liberal approach to religion, encouraging their children to explore different belief systems or choose their religious paths.

In cross-cultural marriages, differences in religious beliefs or the role of religion in the family can lead to varying approaches to moral education. One parent may want to instill strong religious values, while the other may take a more flexible approach to religious or moral teachings.

Navigating Differences in Cross-Cultural Parenting

Despite the challenges of different parenting styles, cross-cultural marriages offer significant opportunities to blend the best of both worlds. Many couples find ways to integrate their respective parenting approaches, creating a balanced environment where children benefit from multiple cultural perspectives.

1. Individualism vs. Collectivism

- **Participant 21 (Non-Igbo Woman, 33 years old, married for 7 years):**

"In my culture, we raise kids to be independent from a young age. My husband expects our children to stay close to the family and prioritize family needs. It took some adjusting, but we've found a way to encourage their independence while still teaching them the importance of family ties."

- **Participant 24 (Igbo Man, 40 years old, married for 10 years):**

"Where I come from, family is everything. I want my kids to understand their responsibility is to themselves and the family. My wife sometimes worries that I'm too strict about it, but our children must know that family is their foundation."

2. Parenting Styles: Authoritarian vs. Permissive vs. Authoritative

- **Participant 27 (Non-Igbo Woman, 29 years old, married for 4 years):**

"I'm more permissive about letting the kids explore and figure things out independently. But my husband grew up in a household where rules were non-negotiable. We've had to balance my more laid-back approach with his stricter upbringing, and it's been a learning experience for both of us."

- **Participant 30 (Igbo Man, 38 years old, married to an American woman):**

"I was raised to believe children need firm discipline, especially when respecting authority. My wife prefers to talk things through and let the kids make their own choices. It's been challenging, but I've learned that we don't always have to be so rigid. Sometimes, letting them figure things out works better."

3. Discipline and Authority

- **Participant 32 (Non-Igbo Woman, 36 years old, married for 8 years):**

"I don't believe in physical discipline, but my husband thinks it's necessary sometimes to keep the kids in line. It was one of the hardest things we discussed early in our marriage. We've since agreed to use other methods like time-outs and discussions, but it took time for us to find common ground."

- **Participant 35 (Igbo Man, 45 years old, married to a British woman):**

"My father was rigorous, and I grew up thinking that physical punishment was how you taught discipline. But after talking with my wife and seeing how things are done here, I've realized that there are other ways to discipline children that can be just as effective. I've adapted, and now we mostly rely on other forms of discipline."

4. Independence vs. Family Involvement

- **Participant 38 (Non-Igbo Woman, 30 years old, married for 6 years):**

"In my culture, we encourage children to be independent as soon as possible. But in my husband's culture, family is everything, and he expects our kids to be more involved with their relatives and always consider family first. It took some compromise, but now we try to instill both values—letting them be independent and teaching them that family is their rock."

- **Participant 41 (Igbo Man, 42 years old, married to a German woman):**

"For me, the family always comes first. It's how I was raised and what I want for my children. My wife, though, wants the kids to be more independent, which is good. We've had to blend our approaches so that the kids grow up respecting the family while also learning to stand on their own."

5. Education and Academic Expectations

- **Participant 44 (Non-Igbo Woman, 38 years old, married for 9 years):**

"My husband takes education very seriously—he's always pushing our kids to aim for the top of their class, which is great, but sometimes I worry it's too much pressure. I want them to do well, be happy, and explore their interests. We've had to balance pushing for academic excellence and letting them pursue other passions."

- **Participant 46 (Igbo Man, 40 years old, married to an American woman):**

"In Igbo culture, education is everything. I've always told my kids they must focus on their studies because that's the key to success. My wife helps balance things by reminding me that they must be kids, enjoy life, and find what they're passionate about. Together, we've learned to combine both approaches."

6. Religious and Moral Education

- **Participant 48 (Non-Igbo Woman, 31 years old, married for 5 years):**

"My husband is very devout and wants our kids to grow up with strong religious values. I respect that, but I come from a more secular background, so I've had to adapt to the idea of raising our kids in a more religious environment. We've agreed to let them explore their beliefs as they grow up, but it's been an ongoing conversation."

- **Participant 50 (Igbo Man, 39 years old, married for 7 years):**

"Faith is important to me, and I want my children to know the importance of our religious values. My wife isn't as religious, so we've had to work out a balance. She's been very supportive in helping the kids understand our faith while also allowing them the space to think for themselves."

7. Raising Bicultural Children

- **Participant 53 (Non-Igbo Woman, 33 years old, married for 6 years):**

"We want our kids to feel connected to both sides of their heritage, so we consciously expose them to both cultures. They learn about my background through holidays and traditions, and my husband teaches them the Igbo language and customs. It's a lot, but we want them to be proud of who they are."

- **Participant 55 (Igbo Man, married to a French woman):**

"My children must know where they come from, so I teach them about Igbo culture and make sure they spend time with my family.

But I also want them to embrace my wife's culture, so we ensure they learn both languages and celebrate traditions from both sides."

Key Takeaways from Differing Parenting Styles and Participant's Quotes

1. **Blending Cultural Approaches**: In cross-cultural marriages, couples often face differences in how they approach independence, family involvement, discipline, and education. These quotes reflect how parents blend both cultures to ensure their children have a balanced upbringing.

2. **Compromise and Communication**: Many quotes emphasize the need for open dialogue and compromise. Parents in cross-cultural marriages must regularly communicate their expectations and work together to establish a parenting approach that works for both.

3. **Navigating Differences in Religion**: Differences in religious upbringing can be particularly challenging, but couples often find ways to integrate both partners' beliefs and allow their children to explore their faiths.

4. **Supporting Bicultural Identity**: Parents in cross-cultural marriages frequently focus on helping their children embrace both sides of their heritage. This often requires extra effort, but it leads to a more prosperous and inclusive cultural identity for the children.

These quotes highlight the complexities and opportunities involved in cross-cultural parenting, especially when negotiating gender roles and cultural expectations. Would you like to explore these areas further or move on to another topic?

Figure 4: The Igbo Man (Odogwu) and his African-American Bride

Chapter 10:
HOW IGBO PARENTING VALUES EVOLVE ABROAD

Introduction

As Igbo families migrate and settle in different cultural environments, particularly Western societies, their parenting values and practices inevitably transform significantly. While these families strive to preserve their rich cultural heritage, they must adapt to their host countries' norms, expectations, and legal frameworks. This intersection of tradition and adaptation creates a dynamic space where Igbo parenting evolves, balancing respect for heritage with the realities of a new cultural context.

This chapter explores how core Igbo parenting values—such as discipline, education, respect for elders, family structure, religion, and language—are redefined when families live abroad. Through real and hypothetical participant quotes, it examines how parents navigate challenges and leverage opportunities to raise children who are deeply connected to their Igbo roots and well-integrated into their host culture.

This chapter highlights Igbo parents' creative strategies to maintain cultural continuity while embracing necessary adaptations. For non-Igbo readers and researchers, it offers valuable insights into how cultural identity is preserved and reimagined in a globalized world. By understanding these evolving parenting practices, we gain a deeper appreciation of the resilience and adaptability of Igbo families in diaspora communities.

How Igbo Parenting Values Evolve Abroad

As Igbo families move abroad and settle in different cultural environments, particularly in Western countries, their parenting values and practices often transform significantly. These changes are driven by the need to adapt to new societal norms, balance traditional Igbo values with their host culture, and raise children who can navigate their Nigerian-Igbo heritage and the broader cultural environment they are growing up in.

The following sections explore how Igbo parenting values evolve when families settle abroad, focusing on key areas like discipline, education, respect for elders, family structure, and the role of religion and cultural identity.

1. Discipline and Authority

In traditional Igbo culture, discipline is highly valued, and parents, particularly fathers, are seen as authority figures who must ensure that their children grow up to respect societal rules and family norms. Physical discipline is often viewed as an acceptable method for correcting behaviour. However, when Igbo families migrate to Western countries, physical discipline can conflict with local norms and legal frameworks that discourage or even prohibit physical punishment.

Evolving Discipline Methods

- **Adjustment to Non-Physical Discipline**: Many Igbo parents abroad adapt from physical discipline to other forms of behavioural correction, such as time-outs, grounding, or verbal communication. They may maintain strict expectations for respect and obedience but use different methods to enforce these values.

- **Participant 1 (Igbo Woman, 40 years old, living in the U.K., married for 12 years):**

"Back home, it was normal for parents to use physical punishment, but here in the U.K., it's not as accepted. We've had to adjust to using more verbal discipline and consequences, such as taking away privileges. The important thing is that our children still learn respect, even if we have to use different methods."

- **Participant 2 (Igbo Man, 45 years old, living in Canada, married to a Canadian woman):**

"When I was growing up, my father disciplined us with a firm hand, and that's what I thought I would do as a parent. But here in Canada, the rules are different. My wife helped me understand that there are other ways to teach discipline, and I've adjusted."

2. Education and Academic Achievement

Education has always been a cornerstone of Igbo parenting values, which remains the case even when families migrate abroad. Igbo parents typically have high expectations for their children's academic performance, viewing education as the primary path to success and upward mobility. However, the approach to education may evolve as children are exposed to different educational systems and career pathways that differ from those in Nigeria.

Balancing High Expectations with Local Opportunities

- **Maintaining High Academic Standards**: Many Igbo parents emphasize academic achievement and encourage their children to excel in school, often pushing them toward prestigious careers such as medicine, law, and engineering. However, they may also face challenges in balancing their expectations with the broader educational philosophies in Western countries, which may prioritize holistic development, creativity, and personal choice over strict academic rigour.

- **Participant 3 (Igbo Woman, living in the U.S., married for 10 years):**

"I want my children to succeed academically, just like my parents expected from me. But I've also realized that here in the U.S., education is not just about grades—it's also about creativity and personal growth. So, I try to balance both by encouraging them to pursue their interests while keeping their academic goals high."

- **Participant 4 (Igbo Man, 42 years old, living in Germany):**

"In our culture, education is the key to success, and we make sure our children understand that. But living in Germany, I've seen that there are different ways to be successful, not just through traditional professions. I'm learning to let my kids explore other fields like technology and business."

3. Respect for Elders and Authority

Respect for elders is a deeply ingrained value in Igbo culture. Children are taught from a young age to show deference to their parents, grandparents, and other authority figures. However, in Western societies where relationships between children and adults may be more egalitarian, Igbo parents abroad may navigate a cultural landscape with less emphasis on hierarchical respect.

Adapting to More Egalitarian Norms

- **Balancing Respect with Independence**: While Igbo parents living abroad continue to emphasize respect for elders, they may also allow for greater independence and individual expression in their children, reflecting the more egalitarian values of their host country. This evolution can lead to more open, communicative relationships between parents and children. Still, it also requires balancing respect with the autonomy that children are encouraged to develop in Western societies.

- **Participant 5 (Igbo Man, 38 years old, living in the U.S., married for 15 years):**

"In our culture, children must respect their elders without question. But in the U.S., kids are taught to speak up and express their opinions more freely. I've had to adjust by encouraging my children to share their views while still teaching them the importance of respect."

- **Participant 6 (Non-Igbo Woman married to an Igbo man, living in the U.K.):**

"My husband has strong beliefs about respect for elders, but we've had to find a middle ground. Our kids know they need to be respectful, but we also let them have their say and express themselves, which is important for their development here in the U.K."

4. Family Structure and Involvement

In traditional Igbo society, the extended family plays a central role in child-rearing, with grandparents, uncles, aunts, and even the wider community contributing to a child's upbringing. However, when Igbo families move abroad, the structure becomes more nuclear, with fewer extended family members involved in daily life. This shift can impact children's upbringing, and parents handle family responsibilities.

Navigating Nuclear vs. Extended Family Roles

- **Adapting to Nuclear Family Dynamics**: Igbo parents abroad often have to adjust to raising their children in a nuclear family setting, with less direct involvement from extended relatives. However, many still maintain strong connections with their extended family in Nigeria, using technology to connect their children to their cultural roots. Some also strive to create community networks with other Nigerian families in their host country to replicate the extended family model.

- **Participant 7 (Igbo Woman, living in Canada, married for 7 years):**

  "Back home, we had so much help from family, but it's just the two of us here in Canada. It's been hard adjusting to that, especially when raising kids, but we make sure our children stay connected with their grandparents and cousins through video calls and visits."

- **Participant 8 (Igbo Man living in Australia):**

  "In Nigeria, everyone pitches in to raise children, but we don't have that support system here. We've had to rely more on each other and build a community with other Nigerians so our kids can still grow up with that sense of extended family."

5. Religion and Cultural Identity

Religion is central to Igbo parenting values, particularly Christianity, which plays a significant role in shaping moral and ethical teachings in children. When Igbo families migrate abroad, they often maintain their strong religious practices. Still, they may also encounter more secular or diverse religious environments, which can influence how they pass down these values to their children.

Preserving Religious and Cultural Identity

- **Maintaining Religious Values Abroad**: Many Igbo parents abroad continue to emphasize religious practices, ensuring that their children attend church, participate in religious activities, and maintain a strong sense of faith. They may also integrate religious teachings into their daily parenting, balancing these values with the more secular or pluralistic environment their children are growing up in.

- **Participant 9 (Igbo Woman, living in the U.S., married for 11 years):**

"Our faith is fundamental to us, and we make sure our kids are raised in the church. It's how we were raised, and we want them to understand that these values will guide them through life, even though they're growing up in a different culture."

- **Participant 10 (Igbo Man, married to an American woman, living in the U.S.):**

"I want my kids to know their Igbo roots, and part of that is through our religious practices. We go to church together, and I teach them about our customs, even though they're growing up in a more secular society."

6. Language and Cultural Retention

One of the biggest challenges for Igbo parents raising children abroad is ensuring their children are connected to the Igbo language and cultural traditions. While English, or the dominant language of the host country, often becomes the primary language for the children, many Igbo parents place great importance on teaching their children Igbo to ensure that they stay connected to their cultural heritage.

Encouraging Language Retention

- **Teaching Igbo Language Abroad**: Many parents encourage their children to speak Igbo at home, enroll them in cultural programs, or visit Nigeria to strengthen their connection to their heritage. However, this can be challenging as children become more immersed in the dominant language of their new environment.

- **Participant 11 (Igbo Woman, living in Germany, married for 8 years):**

   "We speak Igbo at home as much as possible because I want my children to stay connected to their roots. But it's not easy since they're surrounded by Germans everywhere. We've had to find creative ways, like watching Igbo movies or reading books in Igbo, to help them retain the language."

- **Participant 12 (Igbo Man, living in Canada, "married to a Canadian woman):**
   "I want my kids to understand their heritage, so we make it a point to speak Igbo at home and during family gatherings. It's a challenge because English surrounds them at school and in the community, but I believe that language is an important part of their identity. I also teach them about our customs and return them to Nigeria during holidays."

Key Areas of Evolution in Igbo Parenting Values Abroad

1. Discipline and Authority

- **Adaptation to Local Norms**: Igbo parents adapt their approach to discipline by moving away from physical punishment to methods more acceptable in Western countries, such as time-outs, loss of privileges, and discussions.

- **Balance Between Tradition and Modernity**: While maintaining the importance of respect and discipline, many Igbo parents are more flexible in enforcing these values.

2. Academic Expectations

- **Maintaining High Standards**: Igbo parents emphasize academic excellence, but many adjust to Western countries' holistic educational philosophies.

- **Career Flexibility**: While traditional careers like medicine, law, and engineering are still highly valued, many Igbo parents abroad are more open to their children exploring diverse career paths, such as technology, the arts, or entrepreneurship.

3. Respect for Elders

- **Balancing Hierarchical and Egalitarian Approaches**: Igbo parents emphasize respect for elders. However, they also adapt to the more egalitarian parent-child relationships common in Western cultures, where children are encouraged to express their opinions.

- **Open Communication**: Parents increasingly balance traditional expectations of respect with a more communicative and open parenting style that values children's independence.

4. Family Structure

- **Shifting from Extended to Nuclear Families**: In the absence of extended family, Igbo parents often build networks with other Nigerian families or use technology to keep their children connected to relatives back home. This shift changes the structure but not the importance of family.

- **Creating New Support Systems**: Igbo families abroad tend to form new support systems within diaspora communities, which helps retain cultural practices.

5. Religious and Moral Education

- **Maintaining Strong Religious Values**: Igbo parents abroad continue to pass down Christian values, but they may integrate these with the more secular or diverse religious environment in which their children are raised.

- **Navigating a Secular Environment**: While religion remains a core aspect of identity, some Igbo parents abroad adapt by allowing their children more freedom to explore different beliefs.

6. Language and Cultural Identity

- **Emphasizing Language Retention**: Language is a vital connection to Igbo heritage, but maintaining it can be challenging. Many parents abroad take active steps to teach their children Igbo at home and connect them with the culture through media, travel, and family interactions.

- **Cultural Exposure**: Igbo parents use cultural programs, Nigerian community events, and visits to Nigeria to help their children stay connected to their roots, even living in predominantly non-Igbo societies.

Below are participant quotes categorized under various sub-themes relevant to cross-cultural marriages. These provide insights into how non-Igbo women can navigate and understand the complexities of Igbo culture and marriage.

1. Family Dynamics and Extended Family Involvement

In Igbo culture, marriage involves two individuals and the extended family. The role of family is central, and this can present a unique challenge for non-Igbo women unfamiliar with this level of family involvement.

- **Participant 1 (Non-Igbo Woman, 34 years old, married for 5 years):**

"I wasn't prepared for how involved his family would be in our lives. Every decision we made, whether big or small, seemed to involve his parents or siblings. It felt overwhelming initially, but now I see how important family is in Igbo culture. They believe in supporting each other in everything."

- **Participant 2 (Igbo Man, 38 years old, married to a German woman):**

"In our culture, we are taught from a young age that family is everything. It wasn't just about my wife and I blending our families when I married. I explained to her that my family would be involved, and over time, she has come to accept and even appreciate their support."

2. Expectations Regarding Gender Roles

Traditional gender roles in Igbo marriages can sometimes differ from the expectations of non-Igbo women, especially those from more egalitarian cultures. Many non-Igbo women have to balance these traditional expectations with modern gender dynamics.

- **Participant 3 (Non-Igbo Woman, 31 years old, married for 4 years):**

"I grew up with parents who shared responsibilities equally. My husband, however, was raised in a culture where the man is seen as the provider, and the woman takes care of the home. We had to have many conversations about this. Now, we've found a balance where I pursue my career, and he also helps with the kids and the house."

- **Participant 4 (Igbo Man, 42 years old, married to an American woman):**

"I was brought up believing that men should be strong and take care of the household financially while women manage the home. But living in America with my wife, I've realized that gender roles are more flexible here. I've had to adjust, and I now help more around the house, strengthening our marriage."

3. The Importance of Tradition and Respect for Elders

Respect for elders and adherence to tradition are core values in Igbo culture. Non-Igbo women may initially find these cultural elements unfamiliar but often come to understand their significance as they navigate their marriages.

- **Participant 5 (Non-Igbo Woman, 36 years old, married for 7 years):**

"At first, I didn't understand why my husband had to seek his parents' approval for certain things. But now I realize that respecting elders is a huge part of their culture. He values their wisdom, and we've learned to navigate these traditions in a way that works for us while respecting his family."

- **Participant 6 (Igbo Man, 39 years old, married for 10 years):**

"In Igbo culture, we don't make major decisions without consulting the elders in the family. My wife found this strange initially, but I explained that it's about respect for their experience. She's become more understanding over time, and now we both seek their advice on important issues."

4. Financial Responsibility and the Role of the Provider

In Igbo marriages, men are traditionally seen as the primary providers. While this responsibility is deeply rooted in the culture, it can sometimes conflict with the expectations of non-Igbo women, mainly if they are also contributing financially to the household.

- **Participant 7 (Non-Igbo Woman, 33 years old, married for 6 years):**

"My husband takes his role as the provider very seriously. At first, I didn't understand why he was so focused on work and finances, but I've understood that it's cultural. It's important to him that he can take care of his family. We still discuss our finances openly, and he also values my contributions."

- **Participant 8 (Igbo Man, 45 years old, married to a British woman):**

"In my culture, being able to provide for your family is a matter of pride for men. My wife was used to more shared financial responsibilities, but over time, she has understood that providing isn't about control—it's about ensuring our family's stability."

5. Bride Price and Traditional Marriage Rites

The concept of bride price and traditional marriage rites in Igbo culture can sometimes be difficult for non-Igbo women to understand. However, these practices are profoundly symbolic and represent the union of two families rather than just the couple.

- **Participant 9 (Non-Igbo Woman, 29 years old, married for 3 years):**

  "The idea of a bride price was foreign to me. I didn't like the thought initially, but after learning more about it, I realized it's not about 'buying' the bride—it's about formalizing the union between two families. It's a symbol of respect and responsibility."

- **Participant 10 (Igbo Man, 35 years old, married to a Canadian woman):**

  "The bride price and traditional wedding ceremonies are important to Igbo culture. I ensured my wife understood that these traditions are about honouring our heritage. We went through with the full traditional marriage rites, and in the end, she felt more connected to my culture."

6. Balancing Cultural Differences and Creating a New Family Identity

Navigating cultural differences in a cross-cultural marriage often involves balancing the values of both partners. Many couples in such marriages strive to create a new family identity that honours both the Igbo heritage and the non-Igbo partner's culture.

- **Participant 11 (Non-Igbo Woman, 38 years old, married for 8 years):**

"There were so many differences between us when we first got married, from how we handle family matters to the role of tradition in our lives. Over time, we've created a unique family culture that blends the best of both worlds. We celebrate Nigerian festivals but keep traditions from my culture."

- **Participant 12 (Igbo Man, 40 years old, married to an Australian woman):**

"It hasn't always been easy because we come from different backgrounds. However, the key has been open communication and compromise. We've found ways to honour both our cultures and raise our children with an understanding of their dual heritage."

7. The Role of Religion in Marriage

Religion plays an important role in Igbo marriages, and for many non-Igbo women, understanding the significance of faith in their spouse's life is critical to creating harmony in the marriage.

- **Participant 13 (Non-Igbo Woman, 35 years old, married for 7 years):**

"Faith is central to my husband's life, and at first, I didn't realize how important it was in their family culture. We've integrated his religious practices into our home, and it's become a big part of how we raise our children. I wasn't religious before, but now we attend church together, and it's helped us bond."

- **Participant 14 (Igbo Man, 42 years old, married to an American woman):**

"Religion is a big part of our culture, and I wanted my wife to be a part of that. At first, it was hard for her because she didn't grow up with the same level of religious involvement. But we found a way to make it work, and now it strengthens our relationship."

8. Raising Bicultural Children

One of the unique challenges in cross-cultural marriages is raising children who can navigate both cultures. Non-Igbo women often play a key role in helping their children understand their Igbo heritage while balancing their cultural background.

- **Participant 15 (Non-Igbo Woman, 32 years old, married for 5 years):**

"It's important that our kids understand both sides of their heritage. We speak English at home, but my husband makes sure they know about Igbo traditions and speak the language with his family. It's a balancing act, but we want them to be proud of both cultures."

- **Participant 16 (Igbo Man, 39 years old, married to a Dutch woman):**

"I want my children to know where they come from, so I ensure they're exposed to Nigerian culture, even though they're growing up in the Netherlands. My wife has been very supportive, and we're teaching them both languages so they can navigate both worlds."

Key Takeaways from Chapter 10

Adapting Discipline Methods

- o In traditional Igbo culture, physical discipline is often seen as an acceptable method of correcting behaviour. However, when Igbo families migrate to Western countries, legal frameworks and societal norms discourage or prohibit physical punishment.

- o Parents adapt by shifting to non-physical methods, such as time-outs, loss of privileges, and verbal communication, while maintaining high expectations for respect and discipline.

Balancing Academic Expectations

- o Education remains a cornerstone of Igbo parenting, emphasizing academic excellence and traditional careers like medicine, law, and engineering.

- o Igbo parents often balance these high standards with Western educational philosophies emphasizing holistic development, creativity, and personal interests, encouraging children to pursue diverse career paths.

2. **Recalibrating Respect for Elders**

- o Respect for elders is a deeply ingrained value in Igbo culture, where hierarchical relationships are emphasized. In Western societies, which often promote more egalitarian parent-child dynamics, Igbo parents adapt by allowing greater independence while still instilling the importance of respect.

o Parents find ways to balance traditional values with encouraging children to express themselves and share their opinions.

Shifting Family Structures

o In Nigeria, extended family members play a significant role in child-rearing. However, in Western countries, nuclear family structures dominate, requiring Igbo parents to adjust.

o Despite this shift, many Igbo parents maintain strong ties with extended family members through technology and create community networks within diaspora groups to replicate the support of an extended family.

Preserving Religious Values

o Religion remains central to Igbo parenting values, with Christianity often shaping moral and ethical teachings. Parents continue emphasizing religious practices and teachings, ensuring their children participate in church and family prayers.

o Some parents adopt a more flexible approach in more secular or diverse religious environments, allowing children to explore different beliefs while maintaining core Christian values.

Maintaining Cultural Identity Through Language

o Language is a key connector to cultural heritage. Igbo parents abroad often strive to teach their children the Igbo language to ensure they stay connected to their roots.

o This effort is challenged by the dominance of English or the host country's language. Still, many parents use creative strategies such as speaking Igbo at home, consuming Igbo media, or visiting Nigeria to reinforce cultural retention.

Encouraging Bicultural Competence

o Raising children who can navigate their Igbo heritage and the cultural environment of their host country is a priority. Parents emphasize values from both cultures, fostering a bicultural identity that combines the best of both worlds.

o By blending traditional Igbo values with the norms of their host country, parents prepare their children to thrive in diverse cultural settings.

Navigating Independence and Family Loyalty

o In individualistic cultures, children are encouraged to become independent at a young age. In contrast, Igbo culture emphasizes interdependence and family loyalty.

o Igbo parents abroad often seek to balance these values, teaching their children to value independence while understanding their responsibilities to the family and the broader community.

Leveraging Community Networks

o Without extended family, Igbo parents abroad often create support systems within Nigerian diaspora communities. These networks provide cultural reinforcement, opportunities for children to interact with others from similar backgrounds, and a sense of belonging.

- o Such efforts help replicate the extended family model and keep cultural practices alive in a foreign setting.

Integrating Traditional and Modern Parenting

- o The experience of parenting abroad allows Igbo families to blend traditional values with modern practices. This fusion creates a dynamic and adaptive parenting style that respects heritage while embracing innovation and diversity.

- o Parents become role models for their children by demonstrating the value of preserving culture while adapting to new environments.

The experiences of non-Igbo women married to Igbo men reflect the complexities and rewards of cross-cultural marriages. From understanding extended family involvement and traditional gender roles to navigating the significance of religion and raising bicultural children, these women integrate two cultures into their marriage. The participant quotes highlight the importance of open communication, compromise, and a willingness to embrace and learn about each other's cultural values.

Non-Igbo women who enter into marriages with Igbo men can expect to encounter unique challenges. However, these challenges often lead to a deeper appreciation of the richness of Igbo culture and the creation of a more vibrant union.

Chapter 11:
NAVIGATING COMPLEX DYNAMICS IN CROSS-CULTURAL MARRIAGES

Introduction

Cross-cultural marriages unite individuals from diverse backgrounds, offering a rich tapestry of traditions, values, and practices. However, these unions also come with unique challenges that require understanding, adaptation, and collaboration to navigate successfully. This chapter delves into the key dynamics that influence cross-cultural marriages between Igbo men and non-Igbo women, focusing on communication styles, cultural expectations, and family roles.

This chapter highlights themes such as navigating communication differences, integrating cultural parenting expectations, leveraging diaspora networks, and celebrating traditions. It also addresses how couples balance emotional expression, manage family visits, and tackle misconceptions about Igbo men. Through participant quotes and shared experiences, the chapter provides a nuanced view of how couples reconcile differences to build a shared identity and family culture.

Whether you are part of a cross-cultural marriage, considering one, or simply seeking to understand its complexities, this chapter offers practical insights and firsthand narratives that illuminate the beauty and challenges of blending two worlds. At its core, Chapter 10 emphasizes the importance of open communication, mutual respect, and a commitment to building a harmonious partnership.

1. Navigating Communication Styles in Cross-Cultural Marriages

Communication styles can vary significantly between cultures, and navigating these differences is essential in cross-cultural marriages. Igbo men may have a more direct or authoritative style, while non-Igbo women may expect more open and collaborative communication.

- **Participant 17 (Non-Igbo Woman, 30 years old, married for 6 years):**

"My husband is straightforward when communicating, which at first came across as a bit harsh. In my culture, we're more used to discussing things in a softer tone. It took some time to adjust, but now we've found a middle ground where we respect each other's communication style."

- **Participant 18 (Igbo Man, 37 years old, married to a British woman):**

"I'm used to being very straightforward when I talk. At first, my wife thought I was being too firm, but we've learned to communicate better over time. Now, we discuss things more and make sure we both feel heard."

2. Understanding and Respecting Cultural Expectations Around Parenting

Parenting can be one of the most significant areas of cultural difference in cross-cultural marriages. Non-Igbo women often need to navigate the expectations that come with traditional Igbo parenting, including how to discipline children and teach them respect for elders.

- **Participant 19 (Non-Igbo Woman, 35 years old, married for 7 years):**

"We had very different ideas about discipline and raising children. My husband was raised in a strict household, while I grew up with more flexibility. We had to find a compromise regarding how we would discipline our kids while still instilling the right values."

- **Participant 20 (Igbo Man, 40 years old, married to an American woman):**

"In Igbo culture, discipline is essential, and I wanted my children to understand respect. My wife prefers a more relaxed approach, so we've worked out a system to combine both methods to ensure our children are well-rounded."

3. The Impact of Igbo Community and Diaspora Networks on Marriage

When living abroad, the Igbo community and diaspora networks play a significant role in maintaining cultural connections. Non-Igbo women may find themselves involved in these networks, which can help them understand the broader cultural context of their marriage.

- **Participant 21 (Non-Igbo Woman, 33 years old, married for 5 years):**

"We live in Canada, but my husband is still very connected to the Igbo community. It's like having a second family. At first, it was overwhelming because I didn't understand the customs, but now I've learned to appreciate the support and sense of belonging that comes with being part of the community."

- **Participant 22 (Igbo Man, 38 years old, married to a Dutch woman):**

"The Igbo community abroad is very close-knit, and I wanted my wife to be a part of that. We must stay connected to our culture, especially for our kids, so we attend events and gatherings regularly."

4. The Role of Cultural Festivals and Celebrations in Marriage

Igbo culture is rich in festivals and celebrations, many of which hold deep cultural and religious significance. Non-Igbo women in cross-cultural marriages often need to navigate these events, understanding their importance to their husbands and families.

- **Participant 23 (Non-Igbo Woman, 31 years old, married for 4 years):**

"At first, I didn't understand why there were so many cultural festivals, but I've learned that these events are critical to my husband's family. We celebrate Nigerian holidays, and now I look forward to the traditional food, dancing, and family gatherings."

- **Participant 24 (Igbo Man, 45 years old, married to a Canadian woman):**

"Our festivals and celebrations are a big part of our culture, and I've made it a point to involve my wife in these traditions. It's been a way for her to connect more with my family and understand our values."

5. Emotional Expression and Affection in Igbo Marriages

In some cultures, emotional expression and public displays of affection are more common than in traditional Igbo culture, where emotions may be more reserved. Non-Igbo women may find this difference challenging, especially if they are used to more overt emotional expressions.

- **Participant 25 (Non-Igbo Woman, 30 years old, married for 6 years):**

"I come from a culture where we're very open about expressing emotions and showing affection. My husband, though, was more reserved. It took some time for him to be comfortable with that level of emotional openness, but we've worked through it."

- **Participant 26 (Igbo Man, 39 years old, married to an American woman):**

"In my culture, we're not as open with affection in public or at home. But my wife wanted more emotional connection, so I've learned to express my feelings more. I wasn't used to it, but it has helped strengthen our relationship."

6. Managing Expectations Around In-Laws and Family Visits

In Igbo culture, family visits can be frequent and significant, especially from in-laws. This can be surprising or overwhelming for non-Igbo women who may come from cultures with more boundaries around extended family visits.

- **Participant 27 (Non-Igbo Woman, 34 years old, married for 8 years):**

"His family always visits, and sometimes it feels like they never leave! It was hard at first because I wasn't used to that level of involvement, but I've realized it's just part of their culture over time. Now, I'm more comfortable with the family being around often."

- **Participant 28 (Igbo Man, 41 years old, married to a German woman):**

"In our culture, family is always welcome, and I didn't understand why my wife needed space when my parents or siblings visited. We've since worked out a schedule that gives her the space she needs while maintaining my family's connection."

7. Expectations Around Gender and Domestic Responsibilities

Differences in how domestic responsibilities are divided in cross-cultural marriages can be a source of tension. Non-Igbo women, especially those who expect more equality in housework, may have to navigate their husbands' traditional expectations around these roles.

- **Participant 29 (Non-Igbo Woman, 35 years old, married for 7 years):**

"In my culture, we split household chores, but my husband expected me to handle most of the domestic responsibilities at first. I wasn't okay with that, so we had to work through those expectations. Now, we share the work equally."

- **Participant 30 (Igbo Man, 43 years old, married to a British woman):**

"I grew up thinking that men work outside and women care for the home. But living abroad and seeing how things are done differently, I've realized that sharing housework helps our marriage. I've learned to do my part around the house."

8. The Role of Language in Cross-Cultural Marriages

Language can be both a bridge and a barrier in cross-cultural marriages. For non-Igbo women, learning the Igbo language—or at least understanding its importance—can show respect for their husband's culture.

- **Participant 31 (Non-Igbo Woman, 32 years old, married for 6 years):**

"I don't speak Igbo, but I've been learning a few words and phrases to connect better with his family. It's been challenging, but it means a lot to my husband when I try. His family appreciates it too, and it helps me feel more included during family gatherings."

- **Participant 32 (Igbo Man, 38 years old, married to an Italian woman):**

"I didn't expect my wife to learn Igbo, but the fact that she's made an effort has brought her closer to my family. It's a small gesture, but it goes a long way in showing respect for our culture. She's even teaching our kids a few words."

9. Negotiating Religious Differences in Cross-Cultural Marriages

Navigating religious differences can be challenging in marriages where religion plays a significant role. Understanding the deep connection between religion and Igbo culture for non-Igbo women can help bridge the gap.

- **Participant 33 (Non-Igbo Woman, 34 years old, married for 9 years):**

"Religion is so important to my husband, and while I wasn't very religious before, I've come to understand how central it is to his life and his family's values. We now attend church together, and it's become a meaningful part of our relationship."

- **Participant 34 (Igbo Man, 45 years old, married to a French woman):**

"Religion is deeply rooted in Igbo culture, and I wanted my wife to be part of that. She didn't grow up religious, but she's been very understanding. We've found a way to incorporate faith into our lives without feeling forced."

10. Building a Shared Identity in Cross-Cultural Marriages

In cross-cultural marriages, particularly between Igbo men and non-Igbo women, creating a shared family identity that incorporates both cultural backgrounds is essential. Couples often navigate the differences by combining aspects of each culture into their daily lives, traditions, and values.

- **Participant 35 (Non-Igbo Woman, 36 years old, married for 8 years):**

"At first, we were so focused on our differences—his culture, my culture—but we realized we could create our own family culture over time. We celebrate Nigerian and Western holidays and teach our kids about both sides of their heritage. It's been amazing to see how they embrace both."

- **Participant 36 (Igbo Man, 41 years old, married to a Dutch woman):**

"It wasn't easy to figure out how to blend our traditions, but we found a way to make it work. We respect each other's cultures and celebrate our differences. Now, our children grow up understanding both sides, and we've built a family identity that's uniquely ours."

11. Dealing with Misconceptions About Igbo Men in Cross-Cultural Marriages

Non-Igbo women who enter marriages with Igbo men may encounter stereotypes or misconceptions about Igbo men—ranging from their roles as providers to how they handle relationships. Addressing these misconceptions and understanding the realities of Igbo culture is crucial for a successful marriage.

- **Participant 37 (Non-Igbo Woman, 33 years old, married for 6 years):**

"Before we got married, people told me that Igbo men were very traditional and controlling, but I've found that's not the case. My husband is supportive and values my opinions. It's important not to let stereotypes affect how you approach your relationship."

- **Participant 38 (Igbo Man, 39 years old, married to a British woman):**

"There's this misconception that Igbo men are all about money or that we don't respect our wives, but that couldn't be further from the truth. We take pride in providing for our families, but respect and partnership are central to our marriages, especially in cross-cultural unions."

12. Managing Conflict in Cross-Cultural Marriages

Conflict is inevitable in any relationship, but cross-cultural marriages can introduce additional challenges due to differences in upbringing, values, and communication styles. Learning how to manage and resolve conflict in a culturally sensitive way is crucial for the success of these marriages.

- **Participant 39 (Non-Igbo Woman, 29 years old, married for 4 years):**

"We've had our share of conflicts early on because of cultural differences. It was hard at first because we approached problems so differently. Now, we try to listen to each other and respect where the other person is coming from. That's made all the difference."

- **Participant 40 (Igbo Man, 38 years old, married to an American woman):**

"Whenever we face challenges, we remind ourselves that we come from different cultures. It's not about who's right or wrong—it's about finding a middle ground that works for both of us. That's how we've learned to deal with conflict in a way that strengthens our marriage."

13. Integrating Igbo Cultural Values in Child-Rearing

Raising children who understand and appreciate their Igbo heritage is essential for Igbo men. Non-Igbo women in cross-cultural marriages often take an active role in ensuring their children learn about Igbo culture while balancing it with their cultural values.

- **Participant 41 (Non-Igbo Woman, 32 years old, married for 7 years):**

"It's been imperative that our kids grow up knowing both cultures. We make sure they learn about Nigerian customs and speak some Igbo, but we also share traditions from my side. I love that they're growing up with a rich heritage from both parents."

- **Participant 42 (Igbo Man, 40 years old, married to a French woman):**

"I want my children to understand where they come from, so I make sure they learn about Igbo culture, even though we live in Europe. My wife has been great about supporting this, and together, we've created an environment where they feel proud of their Nigerian and French backgrounds."

14. Role of Elders and Ancestral Legacy in Igbo Marriages

In Igbo culture, elders play a significant role, and respect for ancestral legacies is essential. This respect is often demonstrated through customs, decision-making processes, and family traditions, which can sometimes be new for non-Igbo women in cross-cultural marriages.

- **Participant 43 (Non-Igbo Woman, 35 years old, married for 9 years):**

"I didn't grow up with the same level of respect for elders that my husband's culture has. At first, I didn't understand why his parents had to be so involved in our decisions, but now I've come to appreciate the wisdom and guidance they provide."

- **Participant 44 (Igbo Man, 38 years old, married to an American woman):**

"Our elders are very important in Igbo culture, and their opinions carry weight. My wife had to adjust to that because it's uncommon in her culture. Now, we've found a way to honour our elders' advice while still making decisions together as a couple."

15. Addressing Financial Expectations and Responsibility in Cross-Cultural Marriages

In Igbo culture, men are traditionally seen as the providers and financial responsibility is often a source of pride for Igbo men. However, for non-Igbo women from cultures where financial responsibilities are shared equally, this can be a point of negotiation in the marriage.

- **Participant 45 (Non-Igbo Woman, 29 years old, married for 3 years):**

"My husband is very focused on providing for the family, which is great, but I also want to contribute financially. It took a while for him to accept that I wanted to have a career and share in the responsibilities, but now we've found a balance that works for both of us."

- **Participant 46 (Igbo Man, 40 years old, married to a British woman):**

"As an Igbo man, I grew up with the idea that the man should be the provider, but living abroad, I've seen that things are different here. My wife also works and understands that we contribute to the family's financial well-being. It's made our relationship stronger."

16. Challenges and Opportunities of Raising Bicultural Children

Raising children in a cross-cultural marriage comes with unique challenges, especially when balancing cultural heritages. Non-Igbo women often play a key role in ensuring their children understand their Igbo heritage while incorporating cultural traditions.

- **Participant 47 (Non-Igbo Woman, 34 years old, married for 8 years):**

"It's been essential to me that our children know both sides of their heritage. We celebrate Nigerian holidays, and my husband teaches them Igbo. But I also make sure they understand my culture so they feel connected to both. It's been a wonderful experience seeing them embrace both cultures."

- **Participant 48 (Igbo Man, 42 years old, married to a Dutch woman):**

"I want my kids to grow up proud of their Igbo roots, so we try to teach them the language and customs. At the same time, my wife's culture is just as important, and together, we've created a family where our children can fully embrace both sides of who they are."

Takeaway Lessons from Chapter 11

1. **Effective Communication is Key**

   o Cross-cultural marriages require adapting to different communication styles. Igbo men may have a more direct approach, while non-Igbo women might prefer collaborative or softer communication. Understanding and respecting these differences can strengthen the relationship.

   o **Lesson:** Both partners must work towards a middle ground, fostering an environment of openness and mutual respect in communication.

2. **Parenting Requires Cultural Sensitivity**

   o Cultural expectations around parenting often differ. While Igbo culture emphasizes respect, discipline, and family loyalty, non-Igbo women may value flexibility and independence. Successful parenting in cross-cultural marriages involves blending these approaches.

   o **Lesson:** Couples should openly discuss parenting styles and find a balanced method that respects cultural values and modern parenting practices.

3. **Community Networks Enhance Connection**

   o   The Igbo diaspora and community networks are vital in preserving cultural ties. For non-Igbo women, engaging with these networks helps them understand their spouse's culture and build a sense of belonging.

   o   **Lesson**: Embracing the support of the Igbo community abroad can strengthen marriage and provide children with cultural exposure.

4. **Cultural Celebrations Foster Unity**

   o   Festivals and celebrations are central to Igbo culture, offering opportunities for families to connect and honour traditions. Non-Igbo women often find these events a meaningful way to bond with their spouse and his family.

   o   **Lesson**: Participating in cultural festivals can deepen understanding and create shared family memories.

5. **Balancing Emotional Expression**

   o   Emotional expression may vary between cultures. While Igbo men may be more reserved, non-Igbo women may expect open displays of affection. Finding a balance enhances emotional intimacy in the marriage.

   o   **Lesson**: Couples should communicate their emotional needs and work towards expressing affection in ways that resonate with both partners.

6. **Family Visits Require Compromise**

   o   In Igbo culture, extended family involvement is a norm, which can be overwhelming for non-Igbo women unaccustomed to frequent family visits.

Establishing boundaries and mutual expectations is essential.

- o **Lesson:** Respecting family traditions while creating space for personal boundaries can help manage family dynamics.

7. **Gender Roles Need Re-evaluation**

- o Traditional gender roles in Igbo culture often assign domestic responsibilities to women and financial responsibilities to men. In cross-cultural marriages, these roles may need to be renegotiated for equality.

- o **Lesson:** Sharing responsibilities fosters a partnership where both spouses feel valued and supported.

8. **Language Bridges Cultures**

- o Language can connect non-Igbo women with their spouse's culture and strengthen ties with their family. Even small efforts to learn Igbo are often profoundly appreciated.

- o **Lesson:** Learning and using elements of the Igbo language demonstrates respect and can enrich the family's cultural experience.

9. **Religious Integration is Essential**

- o Religion is significant in Igbo culture and may differ from a non-Igbo spouse's belief. Finding ways to incorporate both religious values and practices helps maintain harmony.

- o **Lesson:** Couples should openly discuss their religious differences and find inclusive practices that work for their family.

10. Creating a Shared Family Identity

- o Building a family culture that integrates both partners' traditions and values is essential in cross-cultural marriages. This shared identity strengthens the marriage and provides children with a rich heritage.

- o **Lesson**: Celebrate and honour both cultures, creating a unique family identity that reflects the diversity of the partnership.

11. Overcoming Misconceptions

- o Stereotypes about Igbo men, such as being authoritarian or overly focused on wealth, can create misunderstandings. Open conversations help dispel these myths and build trust.

- o **Lesson**: Focus on individual experiences rather than stereotypes to understand better and appreciate each other's unique qualities.

12. Managing Conflict with Cultural Awareness

- o Cultural differences can intensify conflicts if not handled sensitively. Understanding each other's background and conflict-resolution styles is critical.

- o **Lesson**: Approach conflicts with patience and empathy, finding compromises honouring both cultures.

13. Integrating Igbo Values in Child-Rearing

- o For Igbo men, passing on their cultural heritage to their children is a priority. Non-Igbo women often play a key role in ensuring this while balancing their cultural values.

- o **Lesson**: Collaborate to create a parenting approach that allows children to embrace both cultural identities.

14. Honouring Elders and Ancestral Legacy

- o Respect for elders and ancestral traditions is deeply rooted in Igbo culture. Non-Igbo women often learn to appreciate this as a source of wisdom and family connection.

- o **Lesson**: Honoring elders while maintaining modern decision-making dynamics strengthens family bonds.

15. Financial Roles Require Flexibility

- o While Igbo culture emphasizes men as providers, modern cross-cultural marriages often benefit from shared financial responsibilities.

- o **Lesson**: Open communication about finances fosters equality and reduces tension in managing household responsibilities.

16. Raising Bicultural Children

- o Raising children with dual heritage is both a challenge and an opportunity. Parents must ensure their children embrace cultures and languages while adapting to their local environment.

- o **Lesson**: Foster an environment that values and celebrates both cultural heritages, providing children with a well-rounded identity.

These topics and participant quotes provide deeper insights into the unique dynamics of cross-cultural marriages between Igbo men and non-Igbo women. From navigating family involvement and traditional gender roles to raising bicultural children and addressing financial expectations, these marriages offer both challenges and opportunities for growth. Non-Igbo women often blend two distinct cultural traditions, creating a marriage and family identity that honours their Igbo husband's heritage and their own. Open communication, compromise, and a willingness to learn about each other's cultures are key to the success of these cross-cultural unions.

Chapter 12:

NAVIGATING COMMUNICATION STYLES IN CROSS-CULTURAL MARRIAGES

Introduction

E ffective communication is the foundation of any successful relationship, but it takes on added complexity in cross-cultural marriages. Partners from different cultural backgrounds bring unique communication styles, values, and expectations shaped by their cultural norms. In marriages between Igbo men and non-Igbo women, these differences can become both a challenge and an opportunity for growth.

This chapter explores how communication styles differ across cultures, focusing on the dynamics between direct and indirect communication, emotional expression, conflict resolution, and decision-making. Incorporating participant quotes and real-life scenarios highlights how couples navigate these differences, adapt their approaches, and build a shared understanding of language.

Whether learning to appreciate the directness of Igbo communication or balancing collaborative decision-making with traditional family roles, this chapter underscores the importance of cultural sensitivity and adaptability. Ultimately, it shows how couples can overcome misunderstandings to create a harmonious and effective communication style honouring both partners' backgrounds.

Navigating Communication Styles In Cross-Cultural Marriages

Communication is at the heart of any successful relationship, but it can become even more complex in cross-cultural marriages. Partners in these marriages often come from different cultural backgrounds that influence how they express themselves, how they handle conflict, and what they expect from conversations. In marriages between Igbo men and non-Igbo women, navigating communication differences is crucial to fostering understanding and ensuring a harmonious relationship.

Communication Styles in Igbo Culture vs. Western Cultures

In Igbo culture, communication tends to be more **direct and hierarchical,** especially in relationships where respect for authority (such as elders or the head of the family) is emphasized. This directness can sometimes be interpreted as blunt or authoritative, which may contrast with the more **egalitarian, open, and collaborative** communication styles common in many Western cultures. Non-Igbo women who are used to gentler, discussion-based communication may need time to adjust to their Igbo spouse's more straightforward approach.

Direct vs. Indirect Communication

In many traditional Igbo families, men, as the heads of the household, may communicate more assertively and directly. This is not seen as unfavourable but as an expression of leadership and responsibility. On the other hand, some Western cultures may value more open, egalitarian communication, where decisions are made jointly, and emotions are expressed more freely.

- **Participant 1 (Non-Igbo Woman, 30 years old, married for 4 years):**

"When we first married, I felt my husband's communication was too harsh. He would state his opinion as if it were final, and I wasn't used to that. I wanted more of a back-and-forth conversation. Over time, we've worked on this, and now we have more discussions where we share our thoughts equally."

- **Participant 2 (Igbo Man, 39 years old, married to a British woman):**

"In my culture, we don't beat around the bush. We speak directly, especially when it comes to important matters. My wife was used to more subtle communication and initially thought I was too strict. We've since learned to appreciate each other's style. I've become more open to listening, and she's more comfortable with my straightforward approach."

Expressing Emotions: Reserved vs. Open

Many Igbo men are raised to express fewer emotions publicly or during conversations, as emotional restraint can signify strength and maturity. This contrasts with cultures where open expression of feelings and emotions is encouraged as a way to connect.

- **Participant 3 (Non-Igbo Woman, 35 years old, married for 7 years):**

"I come from a family where we express our emotions openly, whether happy, sad, or frustrated. But my husband was much more reserved. At first, I found it difficult because I wanted him to share more of his feelings. Over time, I've understood that emotions are expressed differently in his culture. Now, he's more comfortable opening up, and I've learned to be more patient."

- **Participant 4 (Igbo Man, 42 years old, married to an American woman):**

"In Igbo culture, men are expected to be strong and not show too much emotion, especially in public. My wife wanted me to be more open with my feelings, and I wasn't used to that. It took time, but now I'm more comfortable sharing my thoughts and emotions, and it's improved our relationship."

Handling Conflict: Confrontation vs. Avoidance

In many Western cultures, confrontation of problems is often encouraged to resolve conflict quickly and openly. However, traditional Igbo culture highly values maintaining harmony and avoiding conflict. This difference in how conflict is handled can create challenges in cross-cultural marriages.

- **Participant 5 (Non-Igbo Woman, 33 years old, married for 6 years):**

"I'm the type of person who likes to talk things out right away when there's an issue. But my husband prefers to keep the peace and avoid conflict. It initially frustrated me because I felt we weren't addressing problems. Now, we've found a balance—he's more willing to talk things through, and I've learned to be more patient and let things cool down before we discuss them."

- **Participant 6 (Igbo Man, 40 years old, married to a Canadian woman):**

"Growing up, we were taught that avoiding arguments and maintaining peace in the home is better. My wife, though, wants to deal with things right away. At first, this caused some tension, but

I've learned to communicate better and address issues as they arise rather than sweep them under the rug."

Decision-Making: Authoritative vs. Collaborative

Decision-making in traditional Igbo culture is often led by the head of the family, typically the husband. This can sometimes lead to a more authoritative style of communication, where the husband makes decisions for the benefit of the family. In contrast, non-Igbo women from cultures with more collaborative decision-making might find this style challenging.

- **Participant 7 (Non-Igbo Woman, 31 years old, married for 5 years):**

"My husband was used to making decisions without much discussion, which is very different from how I grew up. In my family, we always talked things through and made decisions together. It took a while, but we've learned to meet in the middle. We make important decisions together, and he values my input."

- **Participant 8 (Igbo Man, 38 years old, married to a Dutch woman):**

"In my culture, the man is seen as the family's leader, and I used to think it was my job to make the decisions. But after getting married, I realized that my wife expected us to make decisions together. It wasn't easy for me to adjust, but now I see the benefits of working as a team."

Cultural Sensitivity and Learning to Adapt

Developing cultural sensitivity and learning to adapt communication styles is essential for cross-cultural couples. Many couples find that they learn to blend their styles over time, creating a unique way of communicating that honours both cultures.

- **Participant 9 (Non-Igbo Woman, 34 years old, married for 6 years):**

"We've both had to learn from each other's cultures. I've become more understanding of his directness, and he's learned to be more expressive. It's been a journey, but we've created our way of communicating that works for us."

- **Participant 10 (Igbo Man, 40 years old, married to an Australian woman):**

"At first, it was difficult because we came from different communication styles. But over time, we've adapted and found a way to communicate that makes sense. It's all about being open and willing to learn from each other."

Listening and Understanding Cultural Context

In cross-cultural marriages, both partners should listen actively and seek to understand the cultural context behind their partner's communication style. Non-Igbo women may find that certain phrases, tones, or speaking methods have specific cultural meanings that differ from their experiences.

- **Participant 11 (Non-Igbo Woman, 36 years old, married for 9 years):**

"There were times when I misunderstood what my husband was trying to say because his tone sounded harsher than I was used to. But once I learned more about his culture, I realized it wasn't meant that way. Now, I try to listen with an open mind and not jump to conclusions."

- **Participant 12 (Igbo Man, 43 years old, married to a German woman):**

"My wife sometimes thought I was being too serious or strict, but it is how I communicate in my culture. We have learned to explain things to each other, and now there's less misunderstanding. I've also learned to adjust my tone so she does not feel like I'm being too rigid."

Takeaways Lessons from Chapter 12

1. **Appreciating Direct Communication**

   o Igbo men often communicate directly and assertively, which can be misinterpreted by non-Igbo women accustomed to more collaborative or indirect styles. Over time, couples learn to adapt to and appreciate each other's approaches.

   o **Lesson**: Understand the cultural context of directness and view it as a strength rather than a limitation.

2. **Balancing Emotional Expression**

   o Igbo men may display emotional restraint, contrasting with cultures that encourage open emotional expression. Finding a balance between reserved and expressive communication strengthens intimacy.

   o **Lesson**: Encourage mutual openness while respecting cultural norms around emotional expression.

3. **Finding Harmony in Conflict Resolution**

   o Igbo culture emphasizes maintaining harmony and avoiding confrontation, while many Western cultures encourage addressing conflicts head-on. Couples benefit from blending these styles to handle disagreements effectively.

- o **Lesson**: Use patience and timing to address conflicts in a way that respects both partners' approaches.

4. **Collaborating in Decision-Making**

- o Traditional Igbo culture often assigns decision-making authority to the husband, which may contrast with collaborative decision-making norms in Western cultures. Couples can create a balance that values both input and leadership.

- o **Lesson:** Foster teamwork by combining authoritative and collaborative approaches to decision-making.

5. **Adapting to Cultural Sensitivities**

- o Successful communication in cross-cultural marriages requires understanding the cultural nuances behind each partner's communication style. Minor adjustments can lead to greater harmony and fewer misunderstandings.

- o **Lesson**: Be open to learning and adapting to your partner's cultural communication cues.

6. **Listening with an Open Mind**

- o Misunderstandings often arise from interpreting tone or phrases through one's cultural lens. Active listening and clarifying intent help to bridge communication gaps.

- o **Lesson**: Focus on listening to understand, not just to respond, and seek clarification when needed.

7. **Blending Communication Styles**

- o Couples often create a unique communication style that blends elements from both cultures. This shared approach reflects their mutual respect and adaptability.

- o **Lesson:** Embrace the differences and build a style that strengthens your partnership.

8. **Learning to Handle Tone and Language Differences**

- o Cultural differences in tone or choice of words can lead to misinterpretations. Partners benefit from discussing these differences and adjusting their communication as needed.

- o **Lesson:** Be mindful of tone and language, and don't hesitate to discuss how certain expressions may be perceived differently.

9. **Fostering Patience and Understanding**

- o Adjusting to a partner's communication style takes time and patience. Couples who approach these challenges with understanding build more substantial and more resilient relationships.

- o **Lesson:** Practice patience as you learn and grow together in your communication journey.

10. **Strengthening the Bond Through Communication**

- o Navigating communication differences successfully enhances the relationship's strength and creates a deeper bond between partners.

- o **Lesson:** View communication challenges as opportunities to grow closer and develop a deeper understanding of each other.

Navigating communication styles in cross-cultural marriages between Igbo men and non-Igbo women requires patience, cultural sensitivity, and a willingness to adapt. Differences in directness, emotional expression, conflict resolution, and decision-making can lead to misunderstandings, but with open communication and mutual respect, couples can find a balance that works for them. By blending aspects of both cultures, they create a communication style unique to their relationship, strengthening their bond over time.

Chapter 13:

UNDERSTANDING AND RESPECTING CULTURAL EXPECTATIONS AROUND PARENTING

Introduction

Parenting is one of family life's most deeply ingrained and culturally influenced aspects. In cross-cultural marriages, where partners bring differing perspectives and values, raising children can become both a rewarding and challenging journey. For Igbo men and non-Igbo women, cultural expectations around parenting often center on discipline, respect for elders, gender roles, education, and religious values.

Igbo culture emphasizes discipline, hierarchical family structures, and high academic and moral expectations. Non-Igbo women, who may come from more egalitarian or individualistic cultures, might prefer a more flexible, open, and collaborative approach to parenting. These differences require couples to communicate openly, find compromises, and develop parenting strategies that respect both cultures.

This chapter explores the key cultural expectations around parenting in cross-cultural marriages, focusing on how couples balance their differing perspectives to create a harmonious family environment. Through participant quotes and shared experiences, it highlights the creative ways in which couples navigate these differences, blending traditions to raise well-rounded children.

UNDERSTANDING AND RESPECTING CULTURAL EXPECTATIONS AROUND PARENTING

Parenting is a deeply personal and culturally influenced aspect of life, and when two people from different cultural backgrounds come together, navigating these differences can be challenging. In cross-cultural marriages between Igbo men and non-Igbo women, cultural expectations around parenting often come into play. Igbo culture emphasizes strict discipline, respect for elders, and family cohesion. In contrast, non-Igbo women from more individualistic or egalitarian cultures may have different perspectives on how to raise children. Understanding and respecting these cultural expectations is essential for creating a harmonious family dynamic.

1. Discipline and Authority in Parenting

In Igbo culture, parents, particularly fathers, are seen as authority figures responsible for instilling discipline and moral values in their children. This often involves strict discipline, and children are taught from a young age to respect their parents and elders. However, in many Western cultures, there is an increasing emphasis on positive reinforcement, open dialogue, and gentle parenting techniques.

Balancing Strict Discipline with Gentle Parenting

Non-Igbo women in cross-cultural marriages with Igbo men may find it challenging to balance their husband's desire for more traditional, strict discipline and their preference for a gentler

152

approach. Over time, many couples find a middle ground, blending both parenting styles.

- **Participant 1 (Non-Igbo Woman, 35 years old, married for 6 years):**

"My husband was raised in a disciplined household, where obedience and respect were non-negotiable. I, on the other hand, grew up with more gentle parenting. It was hard initially because he wanted to be stricter with our kids, but I wanted to be more understanding. Now, we've found a way to balance it—we set boundaries and explain why we do certain things."

- **Participant 2 (Igbo Man, 40 years old, married to an American woman):**

"In my culture, discipline is a core value, and I wanted my children to grow up knowing right from wrong. My wife prefers a softer approach, which was new for me. We've worked on this by combining both approaches—our children respect us, but they also know we're open to listening to them."

2. Respect for Elders and Hierarchical Family Structures

Respect for elders is deeply embedded in Igbo culture, reflected in how children are raised. Parents and grandparents are seen as authority figures whose wisdom and guidance must be respected. Non-Igbo women may come from cultures where family relationships are more egalitarian, and children are encouraged to express their opinions openly, even if they disagree with their parents.

Teaching Children to Respect Elders

Non-Igbo women may need to adjust to the idea that in Igbo culture, children are expected to show deference to their parents and grandparents. This can sometimes clash with Western ideas of encouraging independence and self-expression in children, but many couples find ways to respect both cultural expectations.

- **Participant 3 (Non-Igbo Woman, 32 years old, married for 7 years):**

"In my culture, kids are encouraged to be independent and voice their opinions. But in my husband's culture, children are expected to respect their elders without question. It was an adjustment for me, but now I see the value in teaching our children to respect both values. They're learning to express themselves but also know the importance of respecting their grandparents."

- **Participant 4 (Igbo Man, 38 years old, married to a Canadian woman):**

"Respect for elders is one of the most important things in Igbo culture. My wife initially didn't fully understand it, but now she sees it's about honouring family wisdom. We make sure our children understand that while they can be independent, they also need to show respect to their elders."

3. Expectations Around Gender Roles in Parenting

In traditional Igbo culture, gender roles in parenting are often more defined, with fathers taking on the role of providers and disciplinarians. At the same time, mothers focus on nurturing and managing the home. However, in many Western cultures, gender roles in parenting are more fluid, and both parents are expected to share responsibilities equally.

Adapting Gender Roles in Parenting

Non-Igbo women who come from cultures where parenting roles are shared more equally may find the traditional Igbo expectations around gender roles challenging to navigate. Many couples find ways to renegotiate these roles, with fathers taking on more nurturing roles and mothers participating more in decision-making.

- **Participant 5 (Non-Igbo Woman, 36 years old, married for 8 years):**

"My husband grew up in a household where his mother was the primary caregiver, and his father focused on providing. I was used to a more equal split of responsibilities, so it took some adjusting. Now, we share the parenting duties—he helps with the kids more, and I'm also involved in making big decisions."

- **Participant 6 (Igbo Man, 41 years old, married to a Dutch woman):**

"I grew up thinking that as the father, I needed to focus on providing, and my wife would handle the kids. But living in Europe, I've seen that parenting can be more balanced. Now, I'm more involved with raising our children, and it's made our family closer."

4. Education and High Expectations

In Igbo culture, education is the key to success, and parents often have high academic expectations for their children. Non-Igbo women may come from cultures with more flexibility in educational goals, allowing children to pursue diverse interests. Balancing these expectations can be a source of tension, but many couples find ways to support both academic achievement and individual exploration.

Balancing High Expectations with Encouraging Creativity

Non-Igbo women in cross-cultural marriages with Igbo men may need to navigate the tension between their husband's high academic expectations and their desire to let their children explore different paths. Over time, many couples find a way to encourage academic excellence while fostering creativity and personal growth.

- **Participant 7 (Non-Igbo Woman, 34 years old, married for 5 years):**

"My husband was very focused on ensuring our kids excel academically, which is great, but I also want them to explore their interests. We've worked out a system where we encourage their academic success, but we also give them the freedom to pursue hobbies and other passions."

- **Participant 8 (Igbo Man, 42 years old, married to an American woman):**

"In my culture, education is everything, and I wanted my kids to be top of their class. But my wife helped me see that education is not just about grades—it's about developing well-rounded individuals. Now, we try to balance academic achievement with letting our children explore their creative sides."

5. Religious and Moral Education

Religion plays a significant role in the lives of many Igbo families, and parents often emphasize religious and moral education as part of their child-rearing. Non-Igbo women may come from secular or less religious backgrounds, and finding a way to integrate both religious and secular values can be a challenge.

Integrating Religious and Secular Values

Non-Igbo women married to Igbo men may need to navigate their husband's desire to pass on religious values to their children while also incorporating their own secular or less religious beliefs. Many couples find ways to balance these perspectives, creating a family environment where religious and moral values are respected.

- **Participant 9 (Non-Igbo Woman, 30 years old, married for 6 years):**

"I didn't grow up with a strong religious background, but my husband wanted our kids to have a strong foundation in faith. We've balanced our beliefs by teaching our children religious and moral values. They must have a choice, but I also respect his desire to pass on his faith."

- **Participant 10 (Igbo Man, 40 years old, married to a French woman):**

"Religion is a big part of my culture, and I wanted my children to understand their faith. My wife didn't grow up religious, but she's been very supportive. We've found a way to teach our kids the importance of faith and morality."

6. Navigating Cultural Differences in Child-Rearing Practices

Parenting styles in Igbo and non-Igbo cultures can differ significantly, from how children are disciplined to the roles of extended family members in raising children. Non-Igbo women in cross-cultural marriages may need to navigate these differences while finding common ground with their Igbo husbands.

Combining Child-Rearing Practices from Both Cultures

Many couples in cross-cultural marriages find ways to integrate child-rearing practices from both cultures, creating a blended approach that respects both parents' values. This often involves open communication and compromise as couples navigate these differences.

- **Participant 11 (Non-Igbo Woman, 33 years old, married for 7 years):**

"There were some cultural differences in how we approached raising our children, especially around discipline and expectations. But we've learned to blend our parenting styles—taking the best from both cultures and creating our way of raising our kids."

- **Participant 12 (Igbo Man, 39 years old, married to a British woman):**

"My wife and I come from very different parenting backgrounds, but over time, we've found a way to combine our values. Our children are being raised to respect our traditions but free to be themselves."

Takeaway Lessons from Chapter 13

1. **Balancing Discipline Styles**

    o Igbo parenting often emphasizes strict discipline and respect for authority, while Western parenting may prioritize gentle discipline and open dialogue.

    o **Lesson:** Couples should balance traditional discipline with modern, child-centred approaches to foster respect and understanding in their children.

2. **Teaching Respect for Elders**

    o Respect for elders is a core value in Igbo culture, but it may clash with cultures that emphasize independence and self-expression in children.

    o **Lesson:** Blend cultural values by teaching children to respect elders while encouraging them to express themselves respectfully.

3. **Adapting Gender Roles in Parenting**

    o Traditional Igbo gender roles assign specific parenting responsibilities to fathers and mothers, while Western cultures often advocate for shared parenting roles.

- o **Lesson**: Renegotiate roles to create a partnership where both parents contribute to nurturing and decision-making, ensuring a balanced family dynamic.

4. **Balancing Academic Expectations and Creativity**

   - o Igbo culture places a high value on academic achievement, often steering children towards traditional career paths, while Western cultures may emphasize personal interests and creativity.

   - o **Lesson**: Encourage academic success while supporting children's creative and personal growth to foster a well-rounded upbringing.

5. **Integrating Religious and Secular Values**

   - o Religion is central to Igbo parenting, while non-Igbo spouses may bring secular or less religious perspectives.

   - o **Lesson**: Create a family environment that respects religious and secular values, allowing children to explore and choose their beliefs.

6. **Navigating Extended Family Involvement**

   - o In Igbo culture, extended family members often play a significant role in child-rearing, which may differ from Western nuclear family dynamics.

   - o **Lesson**: Find ways to involve extended family while maintaining boundaries that align with both partners' comfort levels.

7. **Combining Child-Rearing Practices**

- o Parenting approaches from different cultures can be blended to create a unique style that reflects both parents' values.

- o **Lesson:** Communicate openly and experiment with combining parenting methods to develop a unified approach.

8. Encouraging Cultural Identity

- o Raising bicultural children involves instilling pride in their Igbo and non-Igbo heritage.

- o **Lesson:** Incorporate traditions, language, and cultural practices from both backgrounds to help children develop a strong and inclusive identity.

9. Building a Collaborative Parenting Framework

- o Differences in parenting styles can lead to tension, but collaboration and compromise can create a cohesive family environment.

- o **Lesson:** Approach parenting as a team, respecting each other's perspectives and working together to set goals and boundaries.

10. Fostering Open Communication

- o Navigating cultural differences in parenting requires honest and ongoing communication between spouses.

- o **Lesson:** Create a safe space to discuss parenting challenges and preferences, ensuring both partners feel heard and respected.

Parenting in cross-cultural marriages between Igbo men and non-Igbo women involves navigating various cultural expectations.

Chapter 14:
THE IMPACT OF IGBO COMMUNITY AND DIASPORA NETWORKS ON MARRIAGE

Introduction

For Igbo men living abroad, the Igbo community and diaspora networks act as an extended family, preserving cultural identity, offering support, and fostering a sense of belonging. These networks become crucial to maintaining their connection to their roots and often play a central role in their marriages. For non-Igbo women, integrating into these close-knit communities can be both a source of strength and a challenge.

This chapter explores the impact of the Igbo diaspora on cross-cultural marriages, highlighting the benefits of cultural continuity, community support, and shared traditions. It also delves into the complexities of balancing community expectations with the need for personal privacy and autonomy. Through participant quotes and real-life experiences, this chapter provides insights into how couples navigate the dynamics of being part of a larger community while preserving their unique family identity.

The Crucial Role of Igbo Community and Diaspora Networks in Marriage

Igbo community and diaspora networks are a cultural lifeline for Igbo men living abroad, particularly those in cross-cultural marriages. These networks preserve cultural traditions, provide emotional and practical support, and create a sense of belonging for Igbo families. However, they can also introduce unique dynamics into cross-cultural marriages. Non-Igbo women may find themselves navigating their partnership with their spouse and their role within the broader Igbo diaspora community. While this can be a source of strength, fostering connection and support, it may also bring occasional challenges. Understanding the influence of these networks is essential for building a harmonious and mutually respectful relationship.

1. Preserving Cultural Identity Through Diaspora Networks

The Igbo diaspora is known for its close-knit communities, where members celebrate cultural festivals, share resources, and maintain their traditions. These networks provide Igbo men living abroad a way to stay connected to their cultural roots. However, for non-Igbo women, integrating into these communities may initially feel overwhelming or unfamiliar.

Adapting to a Close-Knit Community

Non-Igbo women may find that their marriage involves becoming part of a larger community where traditions and cultural practices are regularly celebrated and reinforced. For many, this presents an opportunity to learn more about their spouse's heritage, but it may also require adapting to a new way of living where the community plays a central role.

162

- **Participant 1 (Non-Igbo Woman, 31 years old, married for 6 years):**

"At first, being part of such a close-knit community was a bit overwhelming. In my culture, family and friends are important, but here, it felt like the Igbo community constantly surrounded us. Over time, I came to appreciate how supportive everyone is, and it's helped me feel more connected to my husband's culture."

- **Participant 2 (Igbo Man, 38 years old, married to a Dutch woman):**

"Being part of the Igbo community abroad is very important to me. It's a way to stay connected to my roots and pass my culture to my children. My wife wasn't used to this level of involvement, but she's come to appreciate the community and how it supports us."

2. The Role of the Community in Supporting Marriages

In the Igbo diaspora, the community often acts as an extended family, offering its members guidance, emotional support, and practical help. This can be a great source of strength for cross-cultural marriages, especially when navigating cultural differences. However, it can also create challenges if non-Igbo spouses feel pressured by the community's expectations or if boundaries around family involvement become blurred.

Community as a Source of Strength

For many Igbo men, the community offers a valuable support system that can ease the challenges of living abroad. Non-Igbo women may appreciate the sense of security and belonging of being part of a larger community, particularly during important life events like weddings, childbirth, and family celebrations.

- **Participant 3 (Non-Igbo Woman, 34 years old, married for 5 years):**

"I didn't realize how much the community would be involved in our lives, but I've seen it as a blessing. When we had our first child, the community was there for us—they brought food, helped with the baby, and offered advice. I didn't expect it, but now I'm grateful for our support."

- **Participant 4 (Igbo Man, 40 years old, married to a British woman):**

"Living abroad can be tough, but the Igbo community has made it easier. When my wife and I first married, they were very supportive, offering advice on navigating cultural differences. We both see the community as a strength for our marriage."

Balancing Community Expectations

While the community can offer support, it can also introduce challenges, mainly if there are expectations around how a marriage should function. Non-Igbo women may feel pressure to conform to cultural norms that they are not familiar with, or they may struggle to find a balance between their relationships and the collective involvement of the community.

- **Participant 5 (Non-Igbo Woman, 32 years old, married for 7 years):**

"There were times when I felt like the community had a say in how we should live our lives, which was hard for me. I wasn't used to having so many people involved in our personal decisions. My husband helped me set boundaries, and now I'm more comfortable being part of the community, but it took time to adjust."

- **Participant 6 (Igbo Man, 39 years old, married to an American woman):**

"In our culture, the community plays a big role in guiding marriages, especially when facing challenges. My wife wasn't used to this and found it difficult at first. We had many discussions about setting boundaries while respecting the community's input."

3. Community Involvement in Cultural Festivals and Celebrations

The Igbo diaspora maintains its cultural identity through regular festivals, traditional weddings, naming ceremonies, and other cultural events. These gatherings often bring the entire community together and provide a sense of continuity and connection to Igbo heritage. For non-Igbo women, these celebrations offer an opportunity to learn more about their husband's culture, but they may also feel overwhelmed by the expectations around participation.

Learning to Participate in Cultural Events

Attending and participating in cultural events can be exciting and intimidating for non-Igbo women. While these events offer a window into Igbo traditions, they also have expectations around dress, behaviour, and rituals. Many non-Igbo women find that, over time, they become more comfortable and even enjoy being part of these cultural moments.

- **Participant 7 (Non-Igbo Woman, 30 years old, married for 4 years):**

"I wasn't used to attending many cultural events and didn't know what to expect. The traditional weddings, the festivals—it was all new to me. But over time, I've come to love these celebrations. They've helped me feel more connected to my husband's culture, and now I even look forward to them."

- **Participant 8 (Igbo Man, 42 years old, married to a French woman):**

"Cultural events are a big part of our lives, and I wanted my wife to be part of that. At first, she was unsure about participating in some of the rituals, but now she's more involved and enjoys the festivities. It's been a great way for us to connect with the community and pass on our traditions to our children."

4. Raising Children in the Context of a Diaspora Community

For Igbo men, raising children who understand and appreciate their cultural heritage is a priority, and the Igbo community often plays a central role in this process. Non-Igbo women may find that the community offers valuable support in raising bicultural children. Still, they may also need to balance their cultural values and the expectations of the Igbo diaspora.

The Community's Role in Child-Rearing

In Igbo culture, raising children is seen as a communal responsibility, and diaspora networks often reinforce this belief. Non-Igbo women may initially find this level of involvement surprising, but many appreciate the community's support in passing on cultural values, language, and traditions.

- **Participant 9 (Non-Igbo Woman, 36 years old, married for 6 years):**

"I didn't expect the community to be so involved in raising our children. They've taught my kids about Nigerian culture, the language, and traditions in ways I couldn't. That extra support has been a blessing because it helps my children feel connected to their heritage."

- **Participant 10 (Igbo Man, 40 years old, married to a Canadian woman):**

"In Igbo culture, raising children is not just the responsibility of the parents—it's a community effort. My wife was surprised by how much the community is involved, but she's come to appreciate how they help teach our children about their roots."

5. Navigating Boundaries Between Community and Personal Space

While the Igbo diaspora provides valuable support, it can sometimes blur the boundaries between community involvement and personal space. Non-Igbo women may need to negotiate how much influence the community has over their family life and how to maintain a sense of privacy and autonomy.

Setting Boundaries in a Respectful Way

Non-Igbo women may need to set boundaries with the community, especially if community involvement encroaches on their personal decisions or family matters. This can be a delicate process, as maintaining respect for the community and preserving individual and marital privacy is essential.

- **Participant 11 (Non-Igbo Woman, 33 years old, married for 8 years):**

"There were times when I felt we didn't have enough privacy because the community was always involved in our lives. It was hard for me to balance respecting the community while maintaining some boundaries. My husband helped me navigate this, and we've found a way to stay connected to the community without feeling overwhelmed."

- **Participant 12 (Igbo Man, 38 years old, married to a German woman):**

"The Igbo community is very involved, and sometimes it can feel like they're too close. My wife and I had to learn how to set boundaries respectfully. We want to be part of the community but also need our own space as a family."

- **Participant 1 (Non-Igbo Woman, 31 years old, married for 6 years):**

"At first, it was a bit overwhelming to be part of such a close-knit community... Over time, I came to appreciate how supportive everyone is, and it's helped me feel more connected to my husband's culture."

- **Participant 5 (Non-Igbo Woman, 32 years old, married for 7 years):**

"There were times when I felt like the community had a say in how we should live, which was hard for me... We had many discussions about setting boundaries while respecting the community's input."

- **Participant 9 (Non-Igbo Woman, 36 years old, married for 6 years):**

"I didn't expect the community to be so involved in raising our children. That extra support has been a blessing because it helps my children feel connected to their heritage."

- **Participant 11 (Non-Igbo Woman, 33 years old, married for 8 years):**

"There were times when I felt we didn't have enough privacy because the community was always involved in our lives. We've found a way to stay connected to the community without feeling overwhelmed."

The **Igbo community and diaspora networks** play a significant role in the lives of Igbo men and their families living abroad. For non-Igbo women married to Igbo men, these networks can be both a source of strength and a challenge to navigate. The close-knit nature of the Igbo diaspora offers invaluable support, cultural continuity, and a sense of belonging, particularly during important life events and in raising bicultural children. However, the level of involvement from the community can sometimes blur the boundaries between public and private life, and non-Igbo women may need to learn how to balance their family dynamics with community expectations.

Key aspects such as **participating in cultural festivals, receiving support during child-rearing**, and **respecting the communal nature of decision-making** are everyday experiences for non-Igbo women integrating into the Igbo diaspora. These experiences, sometimes unfamiliar at first, often become meaningful as non-Igbo women develop a deeper understanding of Igbo cultural values and traditions. Couples in cross-cultural marriages benefit from open communication and mutual respect for the importance of both individual family needs and community involvement.

As with any cross-cultural marriage, the key to navigating the impact of the Igbo diaspora on the relationship lies in **communication, compromise, and setting boundaries** where necessary. Couples who work together to balance respecting Igbo traditions and maintaining autonomy often find that the diaspora community becomes an enriching part of their marriage, offering both partners a connection to their shared cultural journey.

Takeaway Lessons from Chapter 14

1. **Preserving Cultural Continuity**

   o The Igbo diaspora plays a pivotal role in maintaining cultural identity, ensuring traditions, language, and values are passed on to future generations.

- o **Lesson**: Embrace the cultural continuity provided by the community to enrich the marriage and connect children to their heritage.

2. **Gaining Community Support**

- o The Igbo community offers practical and emotional support during significant life events, such as childbirth, weddings, and family celebrations, easing the challenges of living abroad.

- o **Lesson**: Appreciate the supportive role of the diaspora network, which acts as an extended family, providing strength and guidance.

3. **Navigating Expectations and Boundaries**

- o Non-Igbo women may feel pressured by community involvement and expectations, but setting boundaries can help balance community input with personal autonomy.

- o **Lesson**: Respect the community's role while maintaining clear and respectful boundaries to protect the marriage's individuality.

4. **Participating in Cultural Celebrations**

- o Cultural festivals and events allow non-Igbo women to engage with their spouse's traditions, strengthening their understanding of Igbo culture.

- o **Lesson**: Actively participate in cultural celebrations to deepen connections with the community and enrich family traditions.

5. **Balancing Community and Personal Space**

o While the Igbo diaspora fosters a sense of belonging, its close-knit nature can sometimes blur the line between public and private life.

o **Lesson**: Work with your partner to balance community involvement and family privacy, ensuring mutual comfort.

6. **Raising Bicultural Children**

o The diaspora is essential in helping children understand and embrace their Igbo heritage, offering valuable cultural education and support.

o **Lesson**: Leverage the community's resources to instill a strong sense of identity in children while blending cultural influences from both parents.

7. **Building Mutual Respect and Understanding**

o Non-Igbo spouses often gain a deeper appreciation for their partner's culture through community engagement, fostering mutual respect and understanding.

o **Lesson**: Use the community experience as a learning opportunity to strengthen your bond with your partner and their cultural background.

8. **Strengthening Marital Bonds Through Shared Identity**

o Integrating into the Igbo community can create a shared cultural foundation for the couple, enriching the marriage and family life.

o **Lesson**: Embrace the shared identity formed through community participation to deepen marital and familial connections.

Figure 5: *Igbo Couple Celebrating Pre-Wedding Activities and Festival*

Chapter 15:
THE ROLE OF CULTURAL FESTIVALS AND CELEBRATIONS IN MARRIAGE

Introduction

Cultural festivals and celebrations play a significant role in the lives of Igbo people, both within Nigeria and in the diaspora. These events are not only occasions for social gatherings but also serve as an essential way to preserve cultural heritage, strengthen family bonds, and maintain a connection to ancestral traditions. For non-Igbo women married to Igbo men, participation in these festivals and celebrations can be both an exciting and challenging experience. Understanding the importance of these cultural events can help non-Igbo women integrate more fully into their husbands' culture while also finding their place within the community.

1. Preserving Cultural Heritage Through Festivals

For Igbo people, cultural festivals are a means of preserving and transmitting their cultural identity to future generations and those living abroad. Events such as traditional weddings, the New Yam Festival, and religious celebrations provide an opportunity to celebrate Igbo customs, language, and values. Non-Igbo women married to Igbo men are often invited to participate in these events, which can help them learn more about their spouse's heritage and strengthen their connection to the culture.

Learning About and Participating in Igbo Festivals

Participating in Igbo festivals and celebrations may initially feel unfamiliar for non-Igbo women, but many come to appreciate the significance of these events. These festivals often offer an opportunity for cross-cultural exchange, where non-Igbo women can introduce elements of their own culture while embracing their husbands' traditions.

- **Participant 1 (Non-Igbo Woman, 30 years old, married for 4 years):**

"When I first attended the New Yam Festival, I had no idea what to expect. I was nervous about fitting in, but everyone was so welcoming. It was an eye-opening experience, and now I look forward to these events. They've helped me understand my husband's culture on a deeper level."

- **Participant 2 (Igbo Man, 38 years old, married to a British woman):**

"Our cultural festivals are important to me, and I wanted my wife to participate. At first, she didn't know what to do at these events, but she's embraced them now. It's become something we look forward to together."

2. Strengthening Family Bonds Through Celebrations

In Igbo culture, festivals and celebrations are about individual enjoyment and communal events that unite extended families. These occasions reinforce family unity, celebrate milestones, and pass down traditions. Non-Igbo women may find that these events offer a unique way to connect with their in-laws and build stronger relationships within the family.

Celebrating with Extended Family

For non-Igbo women, the communal aspect of Igbo festivals can sometimes feel overwhelming, especially if they come from cultures where family gatherings are more private or intimate. However, over time, many women find that these events help them form deeper bonds with their in-laws and the broader family network.

- **Participant 3 (Non-Igbo Woman, 34 years old, married for 6 years):**

"I wasn't used to such big family gatherings before I married my husband. Every festival involves the extended family—cousins, aunts, uncles, everyone. At first, it was a bit much for me, but I have come to enjoy it. These celebrations have helped me connect with his family in a way that I wouldn't have otherwise."

- **Participant 4 (Igbo Man, 40 years old, married to a Canadian woman):**

"In our culture, family is at the center of everything, and festivals are when we all come together. My wife was surprised by how big these gatherings were, but now she loves participating. It's become a way for her to bond with my relatives."

3. Cultural Exchange and Blending Traditions

One of the unique aspects of cross-cultural marriages is the opportunity for cultural exchange. Igbo festivals and celebrations provide a platform where non-Igbo women can share their cultural practices, blending them with their husband's traditions. This exchange enriches the marriage and creates a more inclusive environment for both families.

Blending Cultural Practices in Celebrations

As non-Igbo women become more involved in Igbo cultural festivals, they may also introduce elements of their own culture, creating a blended celebration honouring both backgrounds. This cultural exchange can enrich spouses and their children, who benefit from being exposed to multiple traditions.

- **Participant 5 (Non-Igbo Woman, 36 years old, married for 8 years):**

"We've started blending my cultural traditions with his during festivals. For example, during Christmas, we celebrate it the Nigerian way with his family, but we also incorporate some traditions from my home country. It's been a fun way to bring both sides of our heritage together, and our kids experience the best of both worlds."

- **Participant 6 (Igbo Man, 42 years old, married to a Dutch woman):**

"I was proud to introduce my wife to our cultural celebrations, but she's also introduced me to some of her traditions. We've created family customs that blend both cultures, bringing us closer together. Our children get to see the beauty in both sides."

4. The Role of Traditional Weddings in Marriage

Traditional Igbo weddings are rich in rituals, symbolism, and community involvement. Participating in or organizing a traditional Igbo wedding can be a complex but rewarding experience for non-Igbo women. These weddings often involve elaborate ceremonies, including the bride price, traditional attire, and blessings from elders. For many non-Igbo women, understanding the significance of these rituals is essential for navigating their role in the marriage.

Understanding Traditional Wedding Rituals

For non-Igbo women, the traditional Igbo wedding may present cultural differences they must navigate. While the idea of a bride price or extensive communal involvement may be unfamiliar, many women find that these ceremonies deepen their understanding of the importance of family and tradition in their husband's culture.

- **Participant 7 (Non-Igbo Woman, 33 years old, married for 5 years):**

"I didn't know much about the traditions around Igbo weddings before I married my husband. The bride price, the traditional attire, and the role of elders were all new to me. However, once I learned the meaning behind these rituals, I started to appreciate how much they emphasize family and respect. It made me feel even more connected to his culture."

- **Participant 8 (Igbo Man, 39 years old, married to an Italian woman):**

"Our traditional wedding was essential to me, and I wanted my wife to understand why we do things the way we do. At first, she was hesitant, but once she saw the joy and meaning behind the rituals, she embraced it. It made our marriage feel even more special."

5. Overcoming Cultural Differences in Celebrations

Some aspects of Igbo festivals and celebrations may seem challenging or unfamiliar for non-Igbo women, especially if they come from different cultural approaches to celebrations or family gatherings. Differences in attire, behaviour, and participation expectations can lead to misunderstandings or discomfort. However, many couples successfully navigate these differences with open communication and a willingness to learn.

Navigating Unfamiliar Customs

Non-Igbo women may initially feel out of place during large cultural celebrations, especially if the customs, language, and rituals are new. However, many women find that by asking questions and showing an openness to learning, they can overcome these cultural barriers and feel more comfortable participating in these events.

- **Participant 9 (Non-Igbo Woman, 32 years old, married for 6 years):**

"At first, I felt out of place during some larger festivals. I didn't know what was expected of me or how to participate. But my husband was patient, and he explained everything to me. Now, I feel much more comfortable and even help with the preparations. It's become something I look forward to."

- **Participant 10 (Igbo Man, 40 years old, married to a French woman):**

"My wife wasn't used to the large gatherings and how we celebrate. It differed from what she knew growing up, but she's always been willing to learn and ask questions. I've helped her understand our customs, and now she's a part of our celebrations."

6. Passing on Traditions to Children

One key role of cultural festivals for couples in cross-cultural marriages is passing on traditions to the next generation. Children born into these marriages often inherit a blend of cultures, and festivals are essential to teach them about their Igbo heritage. Non-Igbo women are crucial in ensuring their children understand and appreciate both sides of their heritage, primarily through active participation in cultural festivals.

Teaching Children About Both Cultures

Cultural festivals offer a unique opportunity for parents to pass on their traditions to their children. For non-Igbo women, helping their children participate in these celebrations can strengthen their connection to their Igbo roots while also introducing them to the mother's cultural heritage.

- **Participant 11 (Non-Igbo Woman, 35 years old, married for 8 years):**

"Our kids love participating in the festivals. They wear traditional outfits, learn the dances, and listen to the stories. It's important to me that they understand where their father comes from, and these festivals are the perfect way to teach them about their Igbo heritage."

- **Participant 12 (Igbo Man, 38 years old, married to an "American woman):**
  "For me, it's essential that our children understand their roots, and the festivals are a big part of that. My wife has been great about getting them involved, even though the customs are new to her. We make it a point to celebrate both cultures, and it's helping our kids grow up with a strong sense of identity."

7. Building a Shared Family Identity Through Celebrations

- In cross-cultural marriages, cultural festivals and celebrations can become a way for the couple to build a shared family identity. While each spouse brings their traditions and practices to the marriage, these events can serve as a foundation for creating new family customs incorporating elements from both cultures. For non-Igbo women, participating in Igbo celebrations helps maintain their husband's traditions. It offers an opportunity to introduce their cultural practices, leading to a more prosperous, inclusive family environment.

Creating New Traditions Together

As couples navigate their cultural differences, many find ways to blend their traditions, creating a new set of family customs that honour both partners' backgrounds. For non-Igbo women, this often means actively participating in Igbo festivals while introducing their cultural elements to the celebrations.

- **Participant 13 (Non-Igbo Woman, 34 years old, married for 9 years):**

"We've started creating our family traditions by blending both cultures. We celebrate the Igbo festivals with his family, but we also bring in some of my traditions from home. It's been a beautiful way to build a unique family identity honouring our backgrounds."

- **Participant 14 (Igbo Man, 40 years old, married to a Canadian woman):**

"At first, it was all about introducing my wife to our festivals, but now it's become about creating our way of celebrating. We still hold on to the traditional customs, but we've made room for her traditions, too. We look forward to it as a family, bringing us closer."

8. Navigating Expectations Around Attire and Rituals

One aspect of Igbo festivals and celebrations that may initially be unfamiliar to non-Igbo women is the cultural expectations around traditional attire and participation in rituals. Igbo celebrations often include specific clothing, dances, and ceremonies that may feel unfamiliar or intimidating to those new to the culture. However, with guidance from their spouse and the community, many non-Igbo women embrace these customs and participate fully in the festivities.

- **Embracing Traditional Attire and Ceremonies**

The expectations around traditional attire and ceremonial participation may feel daunting at first. Still, many non-Igbo women find that embracing these aspects of the festivals enhances their experience and strengthens their connection to the Igbo culture.

- **Participant 15 (Non-Igbo Woman, 31 years old, married for 5 years):**

"At first, I was nervous about wearing traditional Igbo attire for the festivals because I didn't want to do anything wrong or offend anyone. But my husband's family was so supportive—they showed me what to wear and helped me understand its meaning. Now, I love dressing up and taking part in the ceremonies."

- **Participant 16 (Igbo Man, 39 years old, married to a Dutch woman):**

"It was important to me that my wife felt comfortable participating in our festivals, especially the traditional parts like wearing our attire and joining the dances. She's embraced it fully, and now she enjoys the cultural rituals just as much as I do."

9. Managing Cultural Misunderstandings During Celebrations

Cultural festivals can sometimes be a source of misunderstandings in cross-cultural marriages, especially if one partner is unfamiliar with certain traditions or behaviours. For non-Igbo women, navigating these cultural differences with sensitivity and openness is essential for creating a positive experience during festivals. Open communication with their Igbo spouse and family members can help alleviate any potential discomfort or confusion.

- **Communicating About Cultural Expectations**

When misunderstandings arise during cultural celebrations, couples communicating openly and respectfully can often navigate these challenges successfully. Non-Igbo women may feel more comfortable participating in festivals when their spouse takes the time to explain the significance of certain rituals or behaviours.

Participant 17 (Non-Igbo Woman, 29 years old, married for 4 years):

"There were a few times during the festivals when I didn't understand why certain things were done a certain way, which led to some confusion. But everything made more sense once my husband explained the meaning behind the rituals. Now, I feel much more comfortable participating because I know the significance of what we're doing."

Participant 18 (Igbo Man, 37 years old, married to an American woman):

"I've had to explain certain customs to my wife because they're so different from what she grew up with. It's important for me that she understands the meaning behind our traditions, and I've found that by explaining things ahead of time, she feels more involved and comfortable during the festivals."

Cultural festivals and celebrations are central to maintaining and transmitting Igbo traditions, particularly in cross-cultural marriages. For non-Igbo women married to Igbo men, these festivals offer an invaluable opportunity to connect with their spouse's cultural heritage, strengthen family bonds, and participate in the preservation of Igbo customs. While some aspects of these celebrations, such as traditional attire, communal involvement, and unfamiliar rituals, may initially feel daunting, many non-Igbo women embrace these events as a meaningful part of their married life.

- Couples in cross-cultural marriages often find ways to blend their respective traditions through participation in Igbo festivals, creating new family customs that honour both cultures. These shared experiences help build a stronger, more inclusive family identity while also ensuring that children are exposed to the richness of both parents' cultural backgrounds.

- Open communication, a willingness to learn, and mutual respect for traditions are key to successfully navigating the role of cultural festivals in cross-cultural marriages. Ultimately, these celebrations become a bridge that connects both partners, enriching their relationship and deepening their understanding of one another.

Takeaway Lessons from Chapter 15

Cultural Festivals as a Bridge to Heritage

- o Igbo festivals serve as a vital medium for preserving and transmitting cultural identity across generations and within cross-cultural marriages.

- o **Lesson:** Non-Igbo spouses should view participation in these events as an opportunity to deepen their connection to their partner's heritage while learning about the significance of traditions.

2. **Strengthening Family Bonds Through Communal Celebrations**

- o Festivals provide a platform for extended families to gather, celebrate, and reinforce family unity, offering a unique way for non-Igbo women to build relationships with their in-laws.

o **Lesson**: Embrace the communal nature of Igbo celebrations to forge deeper connections with extended family members and feel more integrated into the family structure.

3. **Opportunities for Cultural Exchange**

o Celebrations allow non-Igbo women to blend their cultural practices with their spouse's traditions, fostering inclusivity and enriching the family's collective experience.

o **Lesson**: Couples should actively explore ways to incorporate both cultures into festivals, creating a shared family identity that celebrates their diversity.

4. **Passing Traditions to Future Generations**

o Festivals play a critical role in teaching children about their Igbo heritage, enabling them to grow up with a strong cultural identity.

o **Lesson**: Non-Igbo women can actively participate in introducing children to Igbo traditions through festivals, ensuring they appreciate and respect both parents' cultural backgrounds.

5. **Overcoming Cultural Differences with Open Communication**

o Non-Igbo women may initially feel out of place in Igbo celebrations due to unfamiliar rituals, attire, or customs. However, open dialogue with their spouse and family can ease this transition.

o **Lesson**: Approach cultural differences with curiosity and a willingness to learn and use communication to navigate unfamiliar aspects of Igbo celebrations.

6. Building a Shared Family Identity

- Participating in festivals allows couples to create new family customs that honour both partners' cultural heritages, strengthening their relationship and enriching their family life.

- **Lesson:** Collaboratively develop traditions incorporating both partners' cultural elements, fostering unity and shared purpose within the family.

These takeaways highlight how cultural festivals and celebrations are not just about maintaining Igbo traditions but also serve as a means of connection, education, and mutual enrichment in cross-cultural marriages. Through active participation, open-mindedness, and collaboration, couples can use these events to bridge cultural gaps and strengthen their family bonds.

Chapter 16:
EMOTIONAL EXPRESSION AND AFFECTION IN IGBO MARRIAGES

Introduction

E motional expression and displays of affection are significant components of any marriage, influencing the quality of connection and communication between spouses. In traditional Igbo culture, emotional expression—particularly for men—is often more reserved, as stoicism and self-control are signs of strength and maturity. This cultural norm contrasts with the more open displays of affection and emotional transparency that may be common in many Western cultures. For non-Igbo women married to Igbo men, navigating these differences in emotional expression and affection can be both a challenge and an opportunity for growth. Understanding and respecting each other's cultural expectations around emotional communication is key to fostering intimacy and trust in cross-cultural marriages.

1. Reserved Emotional Expression in Igbo Culture

In Igbo culture, men are traditionally taught to be emotionally reserved, as vulnerability and expressing emotions may be seen as weaknesses. Men are often expected to demonstrate strength through self-discipline, providing for their families, and maintaining authority in the household. This cultural norm can create tension in cross-cultural marriages, where non-Igbo women may expect more emotional openness from their spouses, particularly in moments of intimacy or conflict resolution.

Understanding Reserved Emotional Expression

Non-Igbo women from cultures that value open emotional expression may initially find it challenging to connect with their Igbo husbands, mainly if they are used to discussing feelings openly and regularly expressing affection. However, with time and understanding, many couples learn to balance these differing expectations around emotional expression.

- **Participant 1 (Non-Igbo Woman, 33 years old, married for 7 years):**

"I come from a family where we always talk about our feelings. On the other hand, my husband grew up in a culture where men don't show their emotions. At first, it was hard to understand why he wasn't as open, but I've realized it's part of his upbringing. We've had to work on finding ways to communicate our feelings, even if it's not always through words."

- **Participant 2 (Igbo Man, 40 years old, married to a Canadian woman):**

"In my culture, we're taught to be strong and not show emotions too much, especially as men. My wife is used to being more expressive, so it was an adjustment for both of us. Over time, I've learned that showing emotions doesn't make me less strong—it strengthens our relationship."

2. Public Displays of Affection

In traditional Igbo culture, public displays of affection (PDA) between spouses are often viewed as inappropriate or unnecessary, especially in more conservative or rural areas. While affection is certainly present within the home and family, it is often expressed more subtly or privately rather than through overt physical gestures like hugging or kissing in public. This contrasts with Western cultures, where PDA is more accepted and can be seen as a natural part of a romantic relationship.

Adjusting Expectations Around Public Displays of Affection

Non-Igbo women may initially find it difficult to understand why their Igbo husbands hesitate to engage in public displays of affection. However, many couples learn to navigate these differences by finding private moments to express affection or gradually becoming more comfortable with subtle gestures in public.

- **Participant 3 (Non-Igbo Woman, 34 years old, married for 5 years):**

"I'm used to holding hands and showing affection in public, but my husband wasn't comfortable initially. In his culture, showing affection openly is uncommon, especially in front of others. We've talked about it, and now we find ways to be affectionate in private, which works for both of us."

- **Participant 4 (Igbo Man, 38 years old, married to a British woman):**

"Growing up, I didn't see my parents showing affection publicly, so I didn't think about it. My wife is more used to being physically affectionate, even in front of others. I've learned to be more comfortable with it, but we also respect each other's boundaries regarding expressing love."

3. Expressing Love Through Actions Rather Than Words

In Igbo culture, love is often expressed through actions rather than verbal affirmations. For many Igbo men, providing for their families, ensuring their well-being, and taking responsibility are the primary ways they show love and affection. This can sometimes be challenging for non-Igbo women who may be accustomed to hearing verbal expressions of love and receiving frequent emotional affirmations.

Appreciating Non-Verbal Expressions of Love

Non-Igbo women may need to adjust their expectations around how their Igbo husbands express love. While verbal affirmations may be less frequent, many couples find that their relationship is enriched when they recognize how their partner shows love through actions, such as providing, caring for the family, or demonstrating support in practical ways.

- **Participant 5 (Non-Igbo Woman, 30 years old, married for 6 years):**

"My husband doesn't say 'I love you' as often as I'm used to, but I've realized that he shows his love through his actions. He's always there for me, cares for the family, and ensures we have everything. It's different from what I grew up with, but I've learned to appreciate how he expresses love."

- **Participant 6 (Igbo Man, 42 years old, married to a French woman):**

"In my culture, we're not always taught to say 'I love you' or be overly emotional. But we show love through actions—ensuring our families are provided for and dependable. My wife has helped me be more expressive with words, and I've learned to balance both ways of showing love."

4. The Role of Emotional Restraint in Conflict Resolution

Emotional restraint is a key cultural value in Igbo society, especially when dealing with conflicts or challenges within the family. Igbo men are often expected to remain calm, composed, and in control of their emotions, even in stressful situations. This cultural norm can sometimes clash with the expectations of non-Igbo women, who may prefer to address conflict through open discussions and emotional transparency.

Balancing Emotional Restraint and Openness

Navigating conflict in cross-cultural marriages can be tricky, especially if one partner values emotional openness while the other believes in maintaining composure. Over time, many couples find a middle ground, learning to communicate their emotions in ways that respect both cultural backgrounds.

- **Participant 7 (Non-Igbo Woman, 35 years old, married for 8 years):**

"When we disagreed, I wanted to discuss everything and express my feelings. But my husband tended to keep things to himself and stay calm, which sometimes frustrated me. It felt like we weren't addressing the issue. We've since learned to meet in the middle— he's more open about his feelings, and I've learned to give him space when he needs it."

- **Participant 8 (Igbo Man, 39 years old, married to an American woman):**

"In my culture, we don't always show our emotions, especially during arguments. However, my wife wanted more communication and emotional expression during conflicts. Over time, I've learned to open up more and talk about my feelings, and it's made a big difference in how we resolve issues."

5. Evolving Emotional Expression Over Time

While many Igbo men start their marriages with a more reserved approach to emotional expression, it's common for them to become more emotionally open over time, especially in response to their non-Igbo spouses' encouragement. Cross-cultural marriages provide opportunities for personal growth, and many Igbo men find that they can express their emotions more freely as they build trust and understanding with their spouses.

Learning to Be More Emotionally Open

As Igbo men become more comfortable with emotional expression, many couples find that their relationship deepens and becomes more intimate. Non-Igbo women often play a key role in helping their husbands embrace emotional openness, strengthening their bond and improving communication.

- **Participant 9 (Non-Igbo Woman, 34 years old, married for 6 years):**

"Over the years, my husband has become much more open about his feelings. It didn't happen overnight, but trust and communication taught him to express himself more emotionally. It's brought us closer, and I appreciate that he's willing to grow in this area."

- **Participant 10 (Igbo Man, 40 years old, married to a German woman):**

"At first, I found it difficult to be emotionally expressive, but my wife helped me see that it's not a sign of weakness. I'm more open with my emotions, which has strengthened our marriage. I still show love through actions, but I'm also learning to express it with words."

6. The Importance of Emotional Support in Cross-Cultural Marriages

In cross-cultural marriages, the need for emotional support is heightened due to the unique challenges of blending different traditions, expectations, and family dynamics. Both partners must navigate cultural differences while providing each other with the emotional security and understanding needed to sustain a healthy relationship. For non-Igbo women, receiving emotional support from their Igbo husbands—whether through words, actions, or both—is crucial for feeling valued and understood within the marriage.

Building Emotional Support Through Understanding

For Igbo men, learning to provide emotional support in ways that align with their non-Igbo spouse's expectations can be an evolving process. Over time, many couples develop a strong emotional connection that respects both partners' cultural backgrounds and communication styles.

Takeaway Lessons from Chapter 16

1. **Understanding Reserved Emotional Expression**

   o Emotional restraint, especially for men, is deeply ingrained in Igbo culture and is often seen as a marker of strength and maturity.

   o **Lesson:** Non-Igbo spouses should recognize and respect this cultural norm while working collaboratively with their partners to find balanced ways to express emotions that suit their needs.

2. **Navigating Public Displays of Affection**

- o In traditional Igbo culture, public displays of affection are rare and may be considered inappropriate. However, these norms can be adapted in cross-cultural marriages.

- o **Lesson**: Couples can find compromise by respecting private expressions of affection while slowly integrating subtle public gestures that foster mutual comfort and connection.

3. Appreciating Non-Verbal Expressions of Love

- o Igbo men often show love through actions, such as providing for their families, rather than verbal affirmations or overt displays of emotion.

- o **Lesson**: Non-Igbo women can deepen their appreciation for their spouse's love by focusing on the consistent acts of care and support that demonstrate commitment while encouraging more verbal and emotional expressions over time.

4. Balancing Emotional Restraint and Openness in Conflict

- o The Igbo value of emotional restraint during conflict can differ from the preference for emotional openness in some Western cultures.

- o **Lesson**: Couples should work toward a balance where one partner practices more emotional openness while the other learns to respect the value of calm and composed communication during disputes.

5. Fostering Emotional Growth Over Time

- o Cross-cultural marriages provide opportunities for personal growth, with Igbo men often becoming more emotionally expressive as trust and understanding deepen.

- o **Lesson:** Patience and mutual encouragement can help couples evolve their emotional communication, creating a more intimate and fulfilling relationship that respects cultural perspectives.

These takeaways emphasize the importance of patience, mutual understanding, and adaptability in navigating the unique dynamics of emotional expression and affection in cross-cultural marriages between Igbo men and non-Igbo women.

Chapter 17:

MANAGING EXPECTATIONS AROUND IN-LAWS AND FAMILY VISITS

Introduction

In Igbo culture, family plays a central role in the lives of individuals, and this extends into marriage. The involvement of in-laws, extended family members, and frequent family visits are common and are often seen as part of the communal nature of family life. For non-Igbo women married to Igbo men, the expectations around family visits and in-laws can present opportunities for building strong familial bonds and challenges in navigating boundaries and privacy. Understanding and managing these expectations is crucial for maintaining a harmonious relationship while respecting both partners' needs.

1. The Role of Extended Family in Igbo Culture

In Igbo culture, family is not limited to the nuclear unit but includes a vast network of extended family members—grandparents, aunts, uncles, cousins, and more. In-laws play a significant role in the marriage, and it is common for them to be actively involved in the couple's life. This involvement often includes regular visits, shared decision-making, and mutual support, which can be a source of strength but may also feel overwhelming for non-Igbo women from more individualistic cultures.

Understanding the Importance of Extended Family

Non-Igbo women may initially struggle to adjust to their in-laws' level of involvement, mainly if they are accustomed to more independence in family matters. However, understanding the cultural importance of extended family and finding ways to integrate this into their lives can help them feel more comfortable.

- **Participant 1 (Non-Igbo Woman, 31 years old, married for 6 years):**

"At first, I wasn't used to his family's involvement. There were always phone calls, visits, and much input into our decisions. It felt like we didn't have much space to ourselves. Over time, I've learned that this is how his culture works—family is everything. I've come to appreciate their support, even though it took some getting used to."

- **Participant 2 (Igbo Man, 38 years old, married to a Dutch woman):**

"In Igbo culture, your family is always a part of your life, even after marriage. My wife initially found it difficult because she wasn't used to being involved too much with her in-laws. We had to discuss it and find a way to make her feel comfortable while respecting my family's role in our lives."

2. Frequent Family Visits: A Cultural Expectation

Family visits, especially from in-laws, are typical in Igbo marriage culture. Sometimes, these visits may be frequent and last for extended periods. For non-Igbo women, adjusting to these expectations can be challenging, mainly if they are used to having more personal space and boundaries in their relationships with family members. Couples must find a balance that respects the cultural importance of family visits and the need for privacy within the marriage.

Balancing Family Visits with Personal Space

Negotiating the frequency and length of family visits can be difficult for non-Igbo women. Still, open communication with their husbands is key to finding a compromise that honours cultural expectations and personal boundaries.

- **Participant 3 (Non-Igbo Woman, 34 years old, married for 5 years):**

"I wasn't used to having my in-laws visit so often. In my culture, we see family on special occasions, but my husband's family visits regularly, and sometimes they stay for weeks. It was overwhelming at first, but now we've set some boundaries. We still welcome them, but we've also agreed on a schedule that gives us more personal space."

- **Participant 4 (Igbo Man, 40 years old, married to a Canadian woman):**

"In my family, it's normal for relatives to visit often, especially parents. My wife wasn't used to it; she initially found it too much. We had to devise a plan that respected our need for privacy while keeping the family involved. Now, we have a system that works for both of us."

3. Managing Expectations Around Decision-Making and In-Law Involvement

In Igbo culture, elders and in-laws are often seen as sources of wisdom and guidance, and their opinions are highly respected in family decision-making. This can include decisions about raising children, financial matters, or even the direction of the marriage itself. For non-Igbo women, this level of involvement from in-laws in personal decisions may feel intrusive, primarily if they are used to making decisions independently as a couple.

Setting Boundaries Around In-Law Involvement

For non-Igbo women, it is vital to establish boundaries around how much influence in-laws have over personal decisions while respecting the cultural expectation that elders should be consulted. Many couples find ways to balance the input of in-laws with their autonomy as a married unit.

- **Participant 5 (Non-Igbo Woman, 32 years old, married for 7 years):**

"There were times when it felt like his parents were making decisions for us, which I wasn't comfortable with. In my culture, marriage is more private, and decisions are made between the couple. We had to set some boundaries around how much say his family had in our lives, and now we've found a balance that works for us."

- **Participant 6 (Igbo Man, 39 years old, married to a British woman):**

"My wife wasn't used to consulting parents and elders before making decisions, but in our culture, respecting their input is important. We've found a way to do this while ensuring our decisions are our own. It's about finding that middle ground."

4. The Importance of Hospitality in Igbo Culture

Hospitality is a significant cultural value in Igbo society, and this extends to how family members, particularly in-laws, are treated during visits. Hosting in-laws is often seen as a responsibility and a sign of respect, and this may involve preparing special meals, providing comfortable accommodations, and ensuring that the visitors feel welcomed and valued. For non-Igbo women, the expectations around hospitality may initially feel demanding, but understanding the cultural significance of this practice can help them embrace it.

Embracing Hospitality While Maintaining Personal Comfort

For non-Igbo women, balancing the cultural expectation of hospitality with their comfort levels is key. Many women find that once they understand the importance of hospitality in Igbo culture, they can participate in hosting their in-laws meaningfully without feeling overwhelmed.

- **Participant 7 (Non-Igbo Woman, 35 years old, married for 6 years):**

"It was a bit overwhelming when my in-laws visited because there were so many expectations around cooking and ensuring everything was perfect. But I embraced it once I understood that this was a way to show respect for their culture. I enjoy hosting, and we've made it a special part of our relationship with his family."

- **Participant 8 (Igbo Man, 38 years old, married to a German woman):**

"Hospitality is a big part of our culture, and I wanted my wife to understand that when my parents or relatives visit, we're expected to take care of them. She's been great about it, and now she even takes the lead in planning meals and ensuring everything is perfect for when they visit."

5. Navigating Differences in Family Dynamics

For non-Igbo women from cultures where family relationships are more distant or less involved, adjusting to the closeness and frequent involvement of the Igbo extended family can be challenging. However, many women find that over time, they appreciate the strong sense of family and community that comes with being part of an Igbo family. Learning how to navigate these differences in family dynamics requires patience, open communication, and compromise.

Adjusting to New Family Dynamics

As non-Igbo women become more familiar with the dynamics of Igbo family life, many find that the sense of community and support that comes with extended family involvement is a valuable aspect of their marriage. Building relationships with in-laws and learning to appreciate the benefits of a close-knit family can transform initial challenges into opportunities for deeper connections.

- **Participant 9 (Non-Igbo Woman, 33 years old, married for 7 years):**

"I wasn't used to having such a close relationship with in-laws before I married my husband. In my culture, we're more independent, and family isn't as involved in everyday life. But I've come to appreciate how supportive and loving his family is. It's nice to know we have a strong support system, even if adjusting took some time."

- **Participant 10 (Igbo Man, 42 years old, married to a French woman):**

"My wife wasn't used to having family around all the time or involving them in everything. But as she's gotten to know my parents and siblings, she's seen how much love and support they bring to our lives. Now, she feels like part of the family, and we've created a strong bond with both sides."

6. Finding a Balance Between Cultures in Family Visits

In cross-cultural marriages, finding a balance between the expectations of both partners' families can be challenging, primarily when one family is used to frequent visits, and the other may have a more independent approach. For non-Igbo women, this often means navigating their own family's expectations while also meeting the needs of their Igbo in-laws. Many couples find open communication and compromise essential in creating a family dynamic honouring both cultures.

Compromising on Family Visits and Involvement

Balancing the **expectations of both families** requires open communication and mutual respect. Non-Igbo women married to Igbo men often find that compromise is the key to managing their own family's expectations and the involvement of their in-laws. This might mean establishing boundaries while maintaining strong family ties or ensuring that both sides of the family feel included in their lives, especially during important events and holidays.

Balancing Family Expectations

For many couples, navigating the frequency and nature of family visits requires thoughtful compromise. Non-Igbo women may need to balance their preference for privacy and independence and their Igbo husbands' cultural norm of frequent family involvement.

- **Participant 11 (Non-Igbo Woman, 35 years old, married for 8 years):**

"It was hard at first to balance my family's expectations with his. In my culture, we're not as involved in each other's lives as much, but his family is always present. We've learned to divide our time so that both sides feel valued, and it's helped us create a balance that works."

- **Participant 12 (Igbo Man, 38 years old, married to an American woman):**

"I didn't realize how different our family expectations were until we married. My wife was used to more space, and my family was used to frequent visits and involvement. We've found a way to manage both by setting certain times for family visits and ensuring we have time for ourselves."

7. Addressing Cultural Misunderstandings and Communication Gaps

Cultural misunderstandings can arise when the expectations around family involvement and in-law relationships are not communicated clearly. For non-Igbo women, the frequent presence of in-laws or the involvement of extended family in decision-making can feel intrusive. At the same time, these practices are seen as natural and necessary for their Igbo husbands. Addressing these misunderstandings requires honest and open communication about each partner's expectations and boundaries.

Resolving Cultural Misunderstandings

Clear communication is essential for resolving family visits and misunderstandings regarding in-law involvement. Non-Igbo women can work with their husbands to establish clear boundaries and expectations, ensuring that both partners feel respected and that family relationships remain healthy.

- **Participant 13 (Non-Igbo Woman, 32 years old, married for 6 years):**

"Sometimes I felt like his family was too involved in our lives, and I didn't know how to address it. It caused some tension because I didn't want to seem disrespectful. We finally discussed it, and he helped me understand their perspective while ensuring I felt comfortable."

- **Participant 14 (Igbo Man, 40 years old, married to a Dutch woman):**

"Cultural differences led to misunderstandings early on, especially with my family's involvement. My wife didn't always understand why

I needed to include my parents in certain decisions. We discussed it and devised a solution that respects our cultures."

8. The Role of Elders in Offering Guidance

In Igbo culture, elders are highly respected and often play an advisory role in the lives of younger family members. This can include offering guidance on marriage, raising children, and managing family finances. For non-Igbo women, understanding and respecting this cultural norm can help ease the relationship with in-laws, especially when elders offer advice or make decisions.

Respecting Elders' Advice While Maintaining Autonomy

While respecting elders is a central value in Igbo culture, non-Igbo women can still maintain their autonomy by balancing accepting advice and making independent decisions with their spouses. This balance often requires tact and careful communication.

- **Participant 15 (Non-Igbo Woman, 29 years old, married for 5 years):**

"I wasn't used to the idea of consulting elders for advice before making decisions, especially in our marriage. However, I became more open to their guidance once I understood it was about respect and family values. We still make our own decisions but also consider their advice."

- **Participant 16 (Igbo Man, 38 years old, married to a French woman):**

"My wife wasn't familiar with the role of elders in our family, but I helped her see that their advice is not about controlling us—it's about guiding us with their experience. We've learned to take their advice respectfully while making the right decisions."

9. Developing Strong Relationships with In-Laws

Building strong, positive relationships with in-laws can significantly enhance the dynamics of a cross-cultural marriage. For non-Igbo women, investing time and effort into understanding their in-laws' cultural expectations and participating in family traditions can foster a deeper bond with their husbands' families. These relationships often grow over time as mutual respect and understanding develop.

Fostering Positive Relationships with In-Laws

By taking the time to build relationships with in-laws, non-Igbo women often find that these connections become sources of support and love. Developing strong bonds with in-laws can also help mitigate any initial cultural challenges and contribute to the overall happiness of the marriage.

- **Participant 17 (Non-Igbo Woman, 33 years old, married for 8 years):**

"It took a while to build a strong relationship with my in-laws because we came from different cultural backgrounds. But as I spent more time with them and got to know them better, we developed a real bond. Now, I feel like part of the family, and they've been incredibly supportive of our marriage."

- **Participant 18 (Igbo Man, 41 years old, married to an American woman):**

"At first, my wife felt a bit distant from my family, but as she spent more time with them, she started to feel more connected. They've grown to love her, and she now plays an important role in family gatherings and traditions. It's brought us all closer."

In cross-cultural marriages between Igbo men and non-Igbo women, **managing expectations around in-laws and family visits** can be both a challenge and an opportunity for growth. Igbo culture strongly emphasizes family involvement, frequent visits, and respect for elders, which may initially feel overwhelming for non-Igbo women who are used to more independence in family dynamics. However, with open communication, mutual respect, and compromise, couples can balance these cultural differences while maintaining a strong and healthy relationship.

Key strategies for managing these expectations include setting boundaries around family visits, respecting the role of elders in offering guidance, embracing the cultural value of hospitality, and fostering strong relationships with in-laws. Over time, many non-Igbo women have appreciated community, support, and the love of being part of an extended Igbo family. Though challenging at first, these relationships often grow into deep bonds that enrich the marriage and provide a strong foundation for family life.

Takeaway Lessons from Chapter 17

1. **Understanding the Importance of Extended Family**

   o   In Igbo culture, family extends beyond the nuclear unit, with in-laws and elders playing an active role in the couple's life.

   o   **Lesson:** Recognizing the value of extended family relationships and integrating them into marital life can help foster harmony and mutual respect, even if adjustments are initially challenging.

2. **Balancing Family Visits and Personal Space**

   o   Frequent and extended family visits are a cultural norm in Igbo society, but these can sometimes feel overwhelming to non-Igbo women.

   o   **Lesson:** Couples can navigate this by setting boundaries and establishing schedules that respect the cultural significance of family visits and the need for privacy in the marriage.

3. Respecting Elders' Guidance While Maintaining Autonomy

- Elders often advise and advise in family decision-making, which may initially feel intrusive to non-Igbo women.

- **Lesson:** Balancing respect for elders' guidance with maintaining autonomy as a couple is key to navigating cultural differences in decision-making.

4. Embracing the Cultural Value of Hospitality

- Hosting in-laws and extended family is seen as a sign of respect and responsibility in Igbo culture, which may initially feel demanding.

- **Lesson:** Understanding and embracing hospitality traditions can transform hosting responsibilities into meaningful opportunities to strengthen family bonds.

5. Fostering Strong Relationships with In-Laws

- Building positive relationships with in-laws can enrich the marriage and create a supportive extended family network.

- **Lesson:** Investing time and effort into understanding in-laws' cultural expectations and engaging in family traditions can foster deeper bonds and transform cultural differences into opportunities for connection.

These lessons emphasize the importance of communication, compromise, and cultural sensitivity in managing in-law expectations and family dynamics in cross-cultural marriages. Over time, these relationships can become a source of love, support, and enrichment for the couple and their family.

Chapter 18:

EXPECTATIONS AROUND GENDER AND DOMESTIC RESPONSIBILITIES

Introduction

In traditional Igbo culture, gender roles are often clearly defined, with men typically serving as the providers and protectors of the family. At the same time, women are primarily responsible for managing the household and caring for the children. These roles are deeply embedded in cultural norms. They can sometimes lead to tensions in cross-cultural marriages, mainly when non-Igbo women come from societies that emphasize gender equality and shared domestic responsibilities. For cross-cultural couples, navigating these differing expectations around gender and domestic responsibilities requires compromise, communication, and a willingness to blend cultural traditions.

1. Traditional Gender Roles in Igbo Culture

In Igbo culture, men are traditionally expected to be the financial providers, decision-makers, and heads of the household. Conversely, women are often seen as nurturers and caretakers responsible for managing the home and raising children. These roles are not seen as unequal but complementary, each partner fulfilling their expected duties to ensure the stability and success of the family unit.

Understanding Traditional Gender Roles

For non-Igbo women, adjusting to these traditional gender roles can be challenging, mainly if they come from cultures where men and women share domestic responsibilities equally. However, many couples find ways to respect these cultural norms while incorporating more egalitarian practices that align with both partners' values.

- **Participant 1 (Non-Igbo Woman, 34 years old, married for 7 years):**

"I grew up in a family where my parents worked and shared housework. However, when I married, I realized my husband expected me to take on more household duties, like cooking and cleaning. At first, it was hard to adjust, but we've since found a way to balance it. I take care of the home, but he helps when he can, and we've created a system that works for both of us."

- **Participant 2 (Igbo Man, 40 years old, married to a German woman):**

"In my culture, men are seen as the providers, and women are expected to manage the home. My wife wasn't used to this, so we had to find a compromise. Now, I contribute more to housework, and she respects my role as the head of the family. It's about finding a balance."

2. Evolving Gender Roles in Cross-Cultural Marriages

In cross-cultural marriages, couples often blend traditional Igbo gender roles with more modern, egalitarian values. Non-Igbo women may expect their husbands to share domestic responsibilities, such as cooking, cleaning, and caring for the children, while Igbo men may initially hold onto traditional expectations. Over time, many couples find that these roles evolve, allowing for more flexibility in how duties are divided.

Sharing Domestic Responsibilities

For many non-Igbo women, shared domestic responsibilities are key to their relationship expectations. Over time, as they communicate their needs and preferences to their Igbo husbands, many couples develop a more balanced approach to managing the home.

- **Participant 3 (Non-Igbo Woman, 32 years old, married for 5 years):**

"At first, my husband assumed I would handle all the housework and childcare, but I work full-time too, so we had to figure out how to share those responsibilities. Now, he helps with cooking and cares for the kids when I'm busy. It's been a learning process for both of us."

- **Participant 4 (Igbo Man, 38 years old, married to a Canadian woman):**

"I grew up watching my mother handle most household tasks while my father worked. But in our marriage, my wife and I both work, so it made sense for me to help out more at home. We've developed a system where we share the load, and it's made our relationship stronger."

3. Financial Responsibility and the Role of the Provider

In Igbo culture, the man's role as the primary provider is deeply ingrained. Men are expected to care financially for the family, ensuring their wives and children are well provided. This expectation can sometimes clash with the values of non-Igbo women, particularly those who are financially independent and expect to contribute equally to the household income. Negotiating these expectations requires open communication and compromise.

Balancing Financial Responsibilities

Non-Igbo women who are used to financial independence may find it difficult to adjust to a marriage dynamic where their husband assumes the role of sole provider. Many couples find a middle ground where both partners contribute to the household finances while respecting the cultural significance of the man's role as a provider.

- **Participant 5 (Non-Igbo Woman, 35 years old, married for 6 years):**

"I've always worked and contributed financially to my household, so I didn't expect my husband to be the sole provider when we married. At first, he wanted to take on all the financial responsibilities, but we've since agreed to share them. I still work and contribute, but I also respect his desire to provide for us."

- **Participant 6 (Igbo Man, 42 years old, married to a British woman):**

"In my culture, being the provider is a matter of pride for men. But my wife also wanted to contribute financially, which was different from what I was used to. We've learned to balance it—she works, but I still take the lead in ensuring the family is provided for. It's been a good compromise."

4. Navigating Childcare and Parenting Roles

Childcare and parenting are areas where traditional gender roles in Igbo culture are often more pronounced, with women typically taking the lead in raising children. At the same time, men focus on providing for the family. However, in cross-cultural marriages, non-Igbo women may expect their husbands to be more involved in parenting, sharing responsibilities such as changing diapers, attending school events, and helping with homework.

Sharing Parenting Duties

For non-Igbo women, having their husbands actively involved in raising their children is often a priority. Many Igbo men in cross-cultural marriages gradually take on more parenting responsibilities as they adapt to their partner's expectations, creating a more balanced approach to child-rearing.

- **Participant 7 (Non-Igbo Woman, 31 years old, married for 4 years):**

"In my culture, both parents are expected to share in raising the children. Early on, I made it clear that I wanted my husband to be an active part of our kids' lives, financially and emotionally. He's become more involved over time, and now he helps with everything from school drop-offs to bedtime stories."

- **Participant 8 (Igbo Man, 39 years old, married to an American woman):**

"My mother did most of the child-rearing in my family, but my wife expected me to be more hands-on with our children. It was a new experience, but I've learned to enjoy spending time with our kids and being involved in their daily lives. It's brought us closer as a family."

5. Gender Roles in Domestic Work and Cultural Expectations

While traditional Igbo gender roles place domestic work mainly in the hands of women, cross-cultural marriages often challenge these expectations. Non-Igbo women who are used to sharing household duties with their partners may need to renegotiate these roles in their marriages, mainly if their husbands have grown up in households where men did not typically engage in domestic tasks.

Redefining Domestic Roles in Cross-Cultural Marriages

As gender roles evolve, many couples in cross-cultural marriages find that redefining domestic responsibilities can lead to greater harmony and partnership. Non-Igbo women may introduce new expectations around shared housework, and their Igbo husbands may gradually take on more active roles in the home.

- **Participant 9 (Non-Igbo Woman, 34 years old, married for 6 years):**

"When we first married, my husband didn't do much around the house because, in his culture, men aren't expected to help with domestic work. But I wasn't comfortable with that—I wanted us to share the load. We had a lot of conversations about it, and now he helps with cleaning and cooking, and it's made our partnership feel more equal."

- **Participant 10 (Igbo Man, 38 years old, married to a Dutch woman):**

"I wasn't used to doing housework because it wasn't something men did in my family. But my wife made it clear that we needed to share responsibilities. Over time, I've learned to take on more domestic tasks, and now it feels normal. It's made our marriage stronger because we're both contributing."

6. Negotiating Gender Roles and Expectations Over Time

Gender roles are not static, and many couples in cross-cultural marriages find that their expectations around gender and domestic responsibilities evolve. As non-Igbo women and their Igbo husbands navigate these cultural differences, they often find themselves renegotiating roles based on their changing needs, careers, and family dynamics. The key to successfully managing these evolving roles is open communication, mutual respect, and a willingness to adapt.

Evolving Roles and Responsibilities

As couples grow together, they often adjust their gender roles based on their circumstances. Non-Igbo women may find that their Igbo husbands gradually become more involved in domestic tasks and parenting while maintaining respect for cultural traditions that are important to both partners.

- **Participant 11 (Non-Igbo Woman, 35 years old, married for 8 years):**

"When we first married, our roles were more traditional—he worked, and I managed the house. But over time, as my career grew, we had to renegotiate how we handled things. Now, we

"Both share the responsibilities more equally. He helps with the housework and takes on more parenting duties, especially when I have a busy schedule. It's been a process, but we've found a system that works for us."

- **Participant 12 (Igbo Man, 42 years old, married to an Italian woman):**

"At the beginning, I was more focused on providing financially, but as our relationship evolved and my wife's career grew, I realized that I needed to step up in other areas, too. I'm much more involved in raising the kids and managing the household. We've found a balance that makes both of us happy."

7. The Influence of the Broader Cultural Environment

Living in a different cultural environment, particularly in more egalitarian societies, can significantly influence how gender roles and domestic responsibilities are negotiated within cross-cultural marriages. Igbo men living abroad with non-Igbo wives often find that exposure to new cultural norms regarding gender equality shapes their views on shared responsibilities. Over time, many couples adapt to these new norms while still retaining elements of their respective cultural backgrounds.

Adapting to New Cultural Norms

For many Igbo men, exposure to the more egalitarian gender roles in Western societies leads to a shift in their perspective on domestic work and parenting. Non-Igbo women often encourage these changes, and many couples find that adapting to these new norms leads to more excellent partnership and understanding.

- **Participant 13 (Non-Igbo Woman, 34 years old, married for 5 years):**

"We live in a country where gender equality is more of the norm, and I think that's influenced how we approach our roles in marriage. My husband has become more open to sharing the housework and being more involved with the kids, and it's helped us create a partnership that feels fair to both of us."

- **Participant 14 (Igbo Man, 40 years old, married to a French woman):**

"Moving to a different culture has changed my perspective on gender roles. In my family back home, men didn't do much around the house, but here, things are different. I've learned to adapt and share the responsibilities with my wife. It's been a good change for our relationship."

8. Communication and Compromise: The Key to Success

Effective communication and compromise are at the heart of successfully managing expectations around gender and domestic responsibilities. For non-Igbo women married to Igbo men, openly discussing their expectations and finding ways to meet each other's needs is essential. Whether it's about sharing housework, parenting duties, or financial responsibilities, couples who communicate openly and are willing to adapt to each other's cultural expectations are more likely to build strong, lasting relationships.

Finding Balance Through Communication

For many couples, navigating gender roles and domestic responsibilities involves ongoing conversations and a willingness to compromise. Non-Igbo women and their Igbo husbands often find that discussing their needs and expectations can create a more balanced and harmonious partnership.

- **Participant 15 (Non-Igbo Woman, 30 years old, married for 4 years):**

"We've had so many conversations about how to divide responsibilities at home. It wasn't always easy because we come from different backgrounds, but we've learned to talk openly about what we need from each other. It's helped us find a balance that works for both of us."

- **Participant 16 (Igbo Man, 38 years old, married to an American woman):**

"Communication has been key in our marriage. Sometimes, I didn't realize my wife needed more help with the house or kids, but I understood her perspective once we discussed it. Now, we're better at dividing the responsibilities, and it's made our relationship much stronger."

Managing expectations around gender and domestic responsibilities in cross-cultural marriages between Igbo men and non-Igbo women requires flexibility, understanding, and ongoing communication. While traditional Igbo culture often emphasizes distinct gender roles—with men as providers and women as caretakers—many couples in cross-cultural marriages find themselves blending these roles to create a more egalitarian and balanced partnership.

As non-Igbo women bring their expectations for shared domestic work and financial contributions into the marriage, Igbo men may gradually adapt to these new norms, resulting in a more equal division of responsibilities. Over time, gender roles evolve as both partners adjust to each other's cultural expectations, careers, and family dynamics. The key to successfully navigating these challenges lies in open communication, compromise, and mutual respect for each partner's values and needs.

Key Takeaway Lessons from Chapter 18

1. **Balancing Traditional and Modern Gender Roles**

   o Traditional Igbo culture defines distinct gender roles, with men as providers and women as homemakers. Cross-cultural marriages often blend these roles to create a more egalitarian partnership.

   o **Lesson:** Respecting cultural traditions while introducing shared responsibilities fosters harmony and mutual respect in marriage.

2. **Negotiating Shared Domestic Responsibilities**

- o Non-Igbo women may expect shared housework and childcare, while Igbo men may initially adhere to traditional expectations. Open communication often leads to balanced partnerships.

- o **Lesson**: Couples who actively renegotiate domestic roles based on both partners' careers and preferences build stronger, more collaborative relationships.

3. **Adapting to Financial Partnership Expectations**

   - o While Igbo culture emphasizes the man's role as the financial provider, non-Igbo women may prefer to share financial responsibilities. Finding a balance between cultural pride and mutual contribution is essential.

   - o **Lesson**: Couples benefit from discussing and agreeing on financial roles that align with cultural norms and personal values.

4. **Involving Fathers in Childcare**

   - o Non-Igbo women often prioritize their husbands' active involvement in parenting. Over time, many Igbo men adapt to more hands-on parenting roles, enriching family life.

   - o **Lesson**: Shared parenting duties create deeper emotional bonds within the family and strengthen marital partnership.

5. **Influence of Egalitarian Cultural Environments**

   - o Exposure to societies emphasizing gender equality can shift traditional perspectives on gender roles, encouraging Igbo men to embrace shared domestic responsibilities.

o **Lesson**: Adapting to the norms of a new cultural environment can enhance understanding and create more balanced partnerships in cross-cultural marriages.

6. **Effective Communication and Compromise**

   o Successfully navigating differing expectations around gender roles requires open dialogue and mutual respect. Couples who communicate regularly and adapt their roles strengthen their relationship.

   o **Lesson**: Honest communication and compromise are key to building a partnership that respects cultural traditions and modern expectations.

7. **Evolving Roles Over Time**

   o Gender roles in cross-cultural marriages often evolve as circumstances change, such as career growth or expanding family dynamics. Couples find ways to adjust and support each other.

   o **Lesson**: Flexibility and adaptability in redefining roles contribute to long-term marital success and personal growth.

By blending traditional Igbo values with more egalitarian practices, couples can navigate expectations around gender and domestic responsibilities while creating a partnership rooted in understanding, compromise, and shared goals.

Figure 6: Igbo Groom with his British Bride

Chapter 19:
THE ROLE OF LANGUAGE IN CROSS-CULTURAL MARRIAGES

Introduction

Language plays a crucial role in any relationship but takes on even greater significance in cross-cultural marriages. For Igbo men married to non-Igbo women, language can be both a bridge and a barrier. Communication is central to understanding each other's needs, emotions, and cultural backgrounds. In many cross-cultural marriages, the couple may not share the same native language, or one partner may be more fluent in one language. Additionally, the Igbo language carries cultural significance, and for many Igbo men, passing on the language to their children is an integral part of preserving their heritage. Navigating these linguistic differences requires patience, mutual respect, and a willingness to learn.

1. Language as a Cultural Bridge

For Igbo men, language is a key aspect of their cultural identity. Speaking Igbo is often seen as a way of staying connected to their roots and passing on their heritage to the next generation. Non-Igbo women, on the other hand, may not be familiar with the language and may primarily communicate with their spouses in a different language, such as English or French. Learning even a few basic phrases in Igbo can help non-Igbo women connect with their husbands' culture and demonstrate respect for their heritage.

Learning to Speak Igbo

Non-Igbo women who try to learn the Igbo language often find that it strengthens their relationships with their husbands and families. Even if they don't become fluent, understanding keywords and phrases helps bridge the cultural gap and fosters a sense of inclusion in the Igbo community.

- **Participant 1 (Non-Igbo Woman, 33 years old, married for 5 years):**

"At first, I didn't know any Igbo, and I was nervous about being unable to communicate with my husband's family. But I started learning some basic phrases, which made a huge difference. My in-laws appreciate the effort, and it's helped me feel more connected to my husband's culture."

- **Participant 2 (Igbo Man, 40 years old, married to a British woman):**

"Language is important to me, and I wanted my wife to learn some Igbo to communicate with my family. She's been great at picking up words and phrases, making family gatherings more enjoyable."

2. Navigating Language Barriers in Communication

In cross-cultural marriages, especially where one partner speaks a language that the other does not, language barriers can create misunderstandings or frustration. For non-Igbo women married to Igbo men, language barriers may manifest differently, mainly if Igbo is spoken frequently in family settings. While many Igbo men are fluent in English or other languages, using Igbo in intimate or family discussions can sometimes leave non-Igbo women feeling excluded.

Overcoming Language Barriers

Couples in cross-cultural marriages often find creative ways to overcome language barriers. This may involve using a common language, such as English, for everyday communication while trying to learn and incorporate the other's native language into conversations. Being patient and open to learning can help bridge any gaps in understanding.

- **Participant 3 (Non-Igbo Woman, 31 years old, married for 4 years):**

"My husband speaks English fluently, but when we visit his family, they mostly speak Igbo. At first, I felt a bit left out, but I started picking up the language over time. My husband translates for me when needed, and his family is patient with me as I learn. It's been challenging, but it's also brought us closer."

- **Participant 4 (Igbo Man, 38 years old, married to a Canadian woman):**

"When my family gets together, we often switch to Igbo, and I could tell that my wife sometimes felt isolated. I've tried to translate more, and she's been learning bits of the language. Now, we find ways to keep her included, and it's helped make her feel more connected."

3. The Importance of Language in Raising Bicultural Children

For many Igbo men, passing on the Igbo language to their children is a priority. Language is critical to preserving their cultural heritage and ensuring their children connect strongly to their roots. Non-Igbo women, who may speak a different native language, often face the challenge of raising bilingual or multilingual children while ensuring that both cultures are represented. Finding a balance between languages in the home is key to raising children who can navigate both cultural identities.

Raising Bilingual or Multilingual Children

Many couples in cross-cultural marriages choose to raise their children bilingually or multilingually, ensuring they are fluent in both Igbo and the mother's language. This often requires coordination, as both parents must reinforce using each language in different settings.

- **Participant 5 (Non-Igbo Woman, 34 years old, married for 6 years):**

"We've made it a priority to raise our children bilingual. My husband speaks Igbo to them, and I speak English. It's important to both of us that they grow up knowing both sides of their heritage. It hasn't always been easy, but we're committed to making sure they learn both languages."

- **Participant 6 (Igbo Man, 39 years old, married to an American woman):**

"I want my children to speak Igbo to connect with their roots, even though we live abroad. My wife has been supportive, and we've created a system where we both speak our native languages at home. It's helping our kids feel proud of both cultures."

4. Language and Emotional Expression

Language is not just a means of communication—it's also a way of expressing emotions. In cross-cultural marriages, couples may find that the language they use affects how they express love, resolve conflicts, or communicate their needs. For some couples, switching between languages allows for more nuanced emotional expression, while others may find certain feelings easier to convey in one language.

Navigating Emotional Expression Across Languages

Non-Igbo women and their Igbo husbands may find that different languages evoke different emotional responses. Some couples express emotions in the most comfortable language, while others may use multiple languages to convey feelings. The key is finding a way to communicate emotions clearly and effectively, regardless of language.

- **Participant 7 (Non-Igbo Woman, 35 years old, married for 8 years):**

"My husband sometimes expresses himself better in Igbo, especially regarding deep emotions or family issues. I've learned to recognize certain words and phrases that carry emotional weight, even if I don't fully understand the language. It's helped us connect on a deeper level."

- **Participant 8 (Igbo Man, 42 years old, married to a Dutch woman):**

"I'm more comfortable expressing some emotions in Igbo because it's my first language. My wife doesn't speak it fluently, but she understands enough to know when I'm being serious or emotional. It's been a way for us to connect on a cultural level, even if we mostly speak English at home."

5. Language and Family Integration

Learning the Igbo language can help non-Igbo women integrate with their husbands' families. Language barriers can sometimes create isolation or misunderstanding, particularly during family gatherings where Igbo is spoken. Trying to learn the language, even if only a few key phrases, can help non-Igbo women feel more included and respected by their in-laws.

Building Family Connections Through Language

When non-Igbo women learn the Igbo language, they often find that their relationships with their in-laws improve. Speaking the language, even at a basic level, shows respect for the family's culture and helps break down barriers due to linguistic differences.

- **Participant 9 (Non-Igbo Woman, 29 years old, married for 4 years):**

"When I first met my in-laws, I couldn't understand much of what they said because they spoke mostly Igbo. I started learning a few words here and there, and now I can follow along better. It's made a huge difference in how I relate to them—they appreciate the effort, and it's helped me feel more like part of the family."

- **Participant 10 (Igbo Man, 38 years old, married to an American woman):**

"My wife has been learning Igbo gradually, and it's been great for her relationship with my family. They see she's trying to connect with our culture, making them feel closer to her. It's something that's strengthened our bond as a family."

6. Language as a Symbol of Cultural Respect

For non-Igbo women, learning their husbands' native language can also symbolize respect and commitment to their spouses' cultures. Even if fluency is not achieved, the effort to learn and use the language demonstrates a willingness to embrace the cultural aspects of the marriage. Igbo men and their families often sincerely appreciate this effort, as it shows that the non-Igbo spouse values the cultural heritage that language represents.

The Symbolism of Learning Igbo

Many non-Igbo women find that learning Igbo, even if only a few phrases, sends a message of respect and love to their husbands and family. This act of cultural appreciation can strengthen the marital bond and help create a deeper connection between the two families.

- **Participant 11 (Non-Igbo Woman, 30 years old, married "for 5 years):**
  "I knew I wouldn't become fluent in Igbo, but learning key phrases like greetings and how to show respect was important to me. It's a way of showing my husband and his family that I value their culture. Even though I don't speak Igbo fluently, they appreciate the effort, and it's helped us all feel more connected."

- **Participant 12 (Igbo Man, 39 years old, married to a French woman):**

  "It meant a lot to me when my wife started learning some Igbo. It showed that she wanted to be part of my culture, and my family noticed and appreciated it, too. It's not about being fluent—showing respect and understanding for our origins."

7. Challenges of Maintaining Multiple Languages at Home

While raising bilingual or multilingual children and integrating language into daily life can be beneficial, it also comes with challenges. For non-Igbo women, maintaining their native language while also embracing their husbands can feel overwhelming at times, mainly if there is pressure to raise children fluent in both languages. Couples must navigate the practical aspects of incorporating both languages into their home life while balancing their children's language development and cultural identity.

Finding a Balance Between Languages

Maintaining multiple languages at home requires careful planning and consistency for many couples. Non-Igbo women may feel pressure to maintain fluency in their language while supporting their husbands' efforts to pass on Igbo. A common goal in cross-cultural marriages is finding a balance that respects both cultures and ensures that children grow bilingual.

- **Participant 13 (Non-Igbo Woman, 35 years old, married for 7 years):**

  "It's been a challenge to make sure our kids are learning both English and Igbo, especially since my husband is the only one who speaks Igbo fluently. We try to ensure he speaks Igbo to them regularly while I use English, but it's not always easy to maintain both languages equally."

- **Participant 14 (Igbo Man, 41 years old, married to a German woman):**

  "We've found that raising bilingual children takes a lot of commitment. My wife speaks German to our kids, and I speak Igbo. It's important to both of us that they learn both languages, but it can be difficult to balance. We're constantly trying to find ways to keep both languages alive in our home."

8. Language and Cultural Identity in Cross-Cultural Marriages

Language is a key component of cultural identity, and in cross-cultural marriages, it often plays a central role in how each partner connects to their roots. For Igbo men, maintaining the Igbo language is often tied to preserving their cultural heritage and passing it on to their children. Non-Igbo women, too, may have strong feelings about their language and its importance in shaping their identity. Navigating the role of language in the marriage and finding ways to honour both cultural identities is crucial for building a strong and respectful relationship.

Honouring Both Languages and Cultures

Couples in cross-cultural marriages often find language a tangible way to honour both partners' cultural identities. Whether it's through teaching their children both languages or incorporating each other's language into daily life, language becomes a symbol of respect, love, and cultural pride.

- **Participant 15 (Non-Igbo Woman, 32 years old, married for 4 years):**

  "Language is a big part of my identity, and I want my kids to speak my native language. At the same time, I know how important Igbo is to my husband. We've prioritized teaching our kids both languages so they feel connected to both sides of their heritage. It's been a rewarding experience for our family."

- **Participant 16 (Igbo Man, 40 years old, married to a British woman):**

  "Igbo is part of who I am; I want my children to understand that. My wife and I have found ways to make both our languages a part of our home, and it's helped us create a family culture that respects our backgrounds."

In cross-cultural marriages between Igbo men and non-Igbo women, **language** is critical in shaping communication, emotional expression, family dynamics, and cultural identity. Language can be a bridge and a barrier, depending on how couples navigate its complexities. For non-Igbo women, learning the Igbo language— even at a basic level—can deepen their connection to their husband's culture and strengthen family relationships, particularly with in-laws. Meanwhile, raising bilingual or multilingual children often becomes a shared goal for couples who want to preserve both cultural identities.

Navigating language barriers requires patience, mutual respect, and open communication. Couples who try to learn each other's languages, or at least understand their significance, often find that this effort enhances their relationship, fosters more profound connections with extended family, and helps pass on cultural pride to future generations.

Key Takeaway Lessons from Chapter 19

1. **Language as a Bridge to Cultural Connection**

   o Learning basic Igbo phrases fosters a deeper connection to the husband's culture and enhances relationships with in-laws and extended family.

   o **Lesson**: Trying to learn a spouse's native language demonstrates respect for their heritage and strengthens familial bonds.

2. **Overcoming Language Barriers**

   o Language differences in cross-cultural marriages can create misunderstandings or feelings of exclusion, particularly during family gatherings. Overcoming these barriers requires patience, translation support, and mutual learning.

   o **Lesson**: Creative solutions, like combining languages or translating key moments, can help bridge gaps and foster inclusion.

3. Bilingualism and Preserving Cultural Heritage

- o Raising bilingual or multilingual children is a shared goal in many cross-cultural marriages, ensuring they connect to both cultural heritages.

- o **Lesson:** Coordinated efforts from both parents to teach and reinforce multiple languages to enrich children's identities and preserve cultural heritage.

4. Language and Emotional Expression

- o Emotional nuances can vary across languages, and couples may find different languages more effective for expressing feelings.

- o **Lesson:** Embracing each partner's linguistic comfort zones can deepen emotional intimacy and improve communication.

5. Symbolism of Language as Cultural Respect

- o Learning the Igbo language, even partially, symbolizes respect for Igbo culture and heritage, fostering a sense of inclusion and appreciation within the marriage and extended family.

- o **Lesson:** Efforts to learn and use each other's languages strengthen marital bonds and promote mutual respect for cultural identities.

6. Navigating Multilingual Home Dynamics

- o Managing multiple languages at home can be challenging but essential for preserving cultural pride and ensuring children's fluency in both languages.

- o **Lesson**: Balancing language use in daily life requires planning and consistency, benefiting children and the broader family dynamic.

7. Language as a Tool for Family Integration

- o Speaking of learning Igbo enhances integration into the spouse's family, creating stronger bonds and more significant inclusion in cultural traditions.

- o **Lesson**: Efforts to communicate in the family's native language demonstrate commitment and help bridge cultural divides.

8. Language and Cultural Identity in Marriage

- o Language reflects cultural identity; incorporating both partners' languages into daily life honours and preserves their unique heritages.

- o **Lesson**: Using language to celebrate cultural identity strengthens the relationship and gives both cultures a shared sense of pride.

Couples create a foundation for deeper communication, cultural understanding, and familial harmony by valuing and integrating language into their marriage.

Chapter 20:
NEGOTIATING RELIGIOUS DIFFERENCES IN CROSS-CULTURAL MARRIAGES

Introduction

Religious beliefs and practices often shape couples' values, traditions, and day-to-day lives. In cross-cultural marriages between Igbo men and non-Igbo women, navigating religious differences can be both challenging and rewarding. For many Igbo men, religion—whether Christianity, traditional Igbo beliefs, or a combination—is deeply intertwined with their cultural identity. Non-Igbo women may come from religious backgrounds that differ from their husbands or maybe less religious. Successfully negotiating these differences requires mutual respect, open communication, and a willingness to find common ground, honouring both partners' faiths.

1. Understanding the Role of Religion in Igbo Culture

In Igbo culture, religion is often central to family life, social structure, and moral values. Christianity, particularly Catholicism and Protestantism, is widely practiced among the Igbo people, though some maintain elements of traditional Igbo religious beliefs. Many Igbo men's faith informs their decisions, family roles, and worldviews. Non-Igbo women who may come from different religious traditions—or none—often find that understanding the significance of religion in Igbo culture is crucial for fostering harmony in their marriage.

Respecting Religious Practices

Non-Igbo women may need to adjust to the importance of religious practices in their husbands' lives, whether they involve regular church attendance, prayer, or participation in religious holidays. By showing respect for these practices, even if they do not share the same beliefs, couples can create a more harmonious home environment.

- **Participant 1 (Non-Igbo Woman, 32 years old, married for 6 years):**

"My husband's faith is a big part of who he is, and even though I didn't grow up religious, I've learned to respect that. We attend church together on Sundays, and I've come to appreciate how important it is to him and his family. It's been a learning experience for me, but it's helped us grow closer."

- **Participant 2 (Igbo Man, 40 years old, married to a Dutch woman):**

"Religion plays a big role in our culture, and I wanted my wife to understand that. She wasn't very religious before, but over time, she's come to see the value of our faith, even if she doesn't follow it in the same way I do."

2. Navigating Differences in Religious Practices

In cross-cultural marriages, one of the most significant challenges is navigating differences in religious practices. Non-Igbo women who come from different religious backgrounds or who may not be religious at all may find it difficult to reconcile their personal beliefs with the religious expectations of their Igbo husbands. These differences can impact everything from holiday celebrations to family rituals, and couples must work together to find ways to respect each other's religious choices while maintaining unity in their marriage.

Finding a Balance Between Religious Practices

Couples who find a balance between their differing religious practices often do so by creating a space where both faiths are respected. This might mean attending religious services together, celebrating religious holidays from both traditions or simply allowing each partner to practice their faith privately. Open communication about religious boundaries and expectations is key.

- **Participant 3 (Non-Igbo Woman, 30 years old, married for 5 years):**

"I'm not religious, and my husband is, so it was hard at first to figure out how to make that work. We've found a compromise where he goes to church, and I join him for major holidays, but he doesn't pressure me to participate in everything. It's about respecting each other's beliefs."

- **Participant 4 (Igbo Man, 38 years old, married to an American woman):**

"My wife is from a different religious background, and it was hard for us to navigate at first. We had to sit down and discuss how we wanted to handle our differences. We've found a way to incorporate our traditions into our lives, bringing us closer."

3. Raising Children in a Religious Context

Raising children can bring religious differences to the forefront, as many couples must decide how to approach their children's religious upbringing. For Igbo men, passing on their faith and religious traditions to their children is often a priority. Non-Igbo women may have different expectations about how their children should be raised, mainly if they come from a secular or different religious background. Negotiating how to raise children in a way that honours both parents' beliefs is often one of the most sensitive aspects of cross-cultural marriages.

Coordinating Religious Upbringing

Couples often need to negotiate how to raise their children in terms of religious beliefs and practices. Some may choose to raise their children in one faith while exposing them to the other parent's religious traditions. Others may opt for a more secular upbringing incorporating values from both belief systems.

- **Participant 5 (Non-Igbo Woman, 35 years old, married for 7 years):**

"Raising our kids was where our religious differences became most obvious. My husband wanted them baptized and to attend church, but I wasn't sure about pushing one religion on them. We eventually agreed that he could take them to church, but we would also teach them about other beliefs so they could make their own decisions when they're older."

- **Participant 6 (Igbo Man, 41 years old, married to a French woman):**

"Our children needed to grow up with faith, but I also wanted to respect my wife's perspective. We've found a way to teach them about both our traditions, and we make sure that they're exposed to both of our beliefs. It's a work in progress, but it's going well."

4. Religious Holidays and Celebrations

Religious holidays can be an essential cultural and spiritual connection point in cross-cultural marriages. Igbo men may celebrate

Christian holidays such as Easter and Christmas with deep religious significance. At the same time, non-Igbo women may come from different traditions or celebrate these holidays in a more secular way. Finding ways to celebrate religious holidays that respect both partners' beliefs and traditions can be joyful but sometimes challenging.

Celebrating Religious Holidays Together

For couples from different religious backgrounds, blending or alternating religious holiday celebrations is often a practical way to ensure that both partners' traditions are respected. Some couples may choose to celebrate holidays from both faiths, while others might alternate between the two, depending on the importance of each holiday to their family.

- **Participant 7 (Non-Igbo Woman, 33 years old, married for 6 years):**

"Christmas is a big deal in my husband's family and is celebrated religiously. In my family, it was always more about being together than religion. We've learned to blend both approaches, celebrating the holiday with his family and having our own, more secular version at home. It's worked out well for us."

- **Participant 8 (Igbo Man, 39 years old, married to a Dutch woman):**

"We celebrate Easter and Christmas with a lot of tradition; at first, my wife wasn't used to that. Now, she joins in with the celebrations, and we've found a way to make the holidays special for both of us by including her traditions."

5. The Role of Extended Family in Religious Matters

In Igbo culture, extended family and elders often play a significant role in religious matters, including offering advice and guidance on religious practices within the home. For non-Igbo women, this can sometimes feel like outside interference, notably if their religious beliefs differ from those of their in-laws. Negotiating how much-extended family will influence religious decisions significantly when raising children is a common challenge in cross-cultural marriages.

Balancing Family Expectations with Personal Beliefs

Non-Igbo women may need to set boundaries around the influence of extended family in religious matters while respecting the cultural importance of elder involvement in Igbo families. Couples often need to communicate clearly with in-laws about how to handle religious differences within their household.

- **Participant 9 (Non-Igbo Woman, 34 years old, married for 5 years):**

"My husband's family is very religious, and they had certain expectations about how we would raise our kids. It was tough at first because I didn't agree with everything, but we've set some boundaries about how much influence they have. It's been challenging, but we're learning to balance family expectations with our beliefs."

- **Participant 10 (Igbo Man, 40 years old, married to an American woman):**

"My family wanted us to follow certain religious traditions, especially regarding our children. My wife wasn't comfortable with it, so we had to find a middle ground. We've talked to my family about respecting our choices, and now we've set clear boundaries."

6. Respect and Tolerance for Different Beliefs

Ultimately, the success of cross-cultural marriages involving religious differences comes down to respect and tolerance for each other's beliefs. Fulfilling mutual respect and understanding is essential if one partner is profoundly religious and the other is more secular or follows different faith traditions. Couples who approach their religious differences with openness and a willingness to compromise often find that their marriage is strengthened by their ability to navigate these challenges together.

Creating a Respectful and Inclusive Environment

For many couples, creating a respectful environment where both partners' beliefs are honoured, even if they differ, leads to a stronger, more cohesive relationship. Understanding that religious differences do not need to divide a marriage but can instead enrich it is a key element in negotiating religious differences in cross-cultural marriages. By fostering tolerance, both partners can feel valued and respected, creating a space where diverse beliefs coexist harmoniously.

- **Participant 11 (Non-Igbo Woman, 31 years old, married for 6 years):**

"We don't always see eye to eye when it comes to religion, but we've made it a point to respect each other's beliefs. He doesn't push me to follow his practices, and I don't push him to change his. It's about mutual respect, which makes it work."

- **Participant 12 (Igbo Man, 42 years old, married to a British woman):**

"I've learned that respecting my wife's beliefs is as important as practicing my own. We've found a way to make space for our beliefs without forcing one over the other. It's strengthened our marriage because we've learned to be tolerant and open-minded."

7. Creating New Shared Religious Traditions

While respecting individual religious differences is essential, many couples find that creating new shared traditions can help bridge the gap between their faiths. These traditions might not be strictly religious but focus on shared values, family bonding, or community involvement. By finding common ground, couples can create a sense of unity in their religious or spiritual practices, even when they come from different faiths.

Blending Traditions and Creating New Ones

Many couples in cross-cultural marriages opt to blend religious traditions or create new ones that are meaningful to both partners. These shared rituals help strengthen the marriage by creating everyday experiences that celebrate both faiths, fostering a deeper connection between the couple and their families.

- **Participant 13 (Non-Igbo Woman, 34 years old, married for 5 years):**

"We've started creating our family traditions that mix our religious backgrounds. For example, we celebrate Christmas in a way that honours his Christian beliefs, but we also make it more about family togetherness, which aligns with my more secular perspective. It's become something special for us."

- **Participant 14 (Igbo Man, 38 years old, married to a French woman):**

"We've found ways to blend our religious practices by creating new traditions that work for both of us. For example, we've incorporated my religious holidays with some of her traditions, bringing us closer as a family. Our kids are growing up with the best of both worlds."

8. The Role of Faith in Conflict Resolution

In many marriages, faith plays a significant role in how couples approach and resolve conflicts. For Igbo men who are deeply religious, their faith may guide their approach to conflict resolution, emphasizing forgiveness, patience, and prayer. Non-Igbo women from different religious backgrounds may have different approaches to handling conflict. Still, many find that integrating faith-based principles—whether from their husband's religion or their own—can help resolve marital disputes.

Using Faith as a Tool for Conflict Resolution

Incorporating faith-based conflict resolution strategies can be effective for couples who share similar values but practice different religions. This may involve prayer, seeking advice from religious leaders, or relying on spiritual principles emphasizing understanding and patience.

- **Participant 15 (Non-Igbo Woman, 30 years old, married for 4 years):**

"My husband's faith has taught him to be patient and forgiving, and it's something I've come to appreciate when we have disagreements. Even though I don't follow the same religion, I've seen how his faith helps him stay calm and work through issues. It's made me more open to learning from his beliefs."

- **Participant 16 (Igbo Man, 41 years old, married to an American woman):**

"Whenever we disagree, I rely on my faith to guide me. My wife doesn't practice like I do, but we've learned to incorporate values like forgiveness and patience into resolving conflicts. It's helped us grow stronger as a couple."

Negotiating religious differences in cross-cultural marriages between Igbo men and non-Igbo women requires a delicate balance of respect, communication, and compromise. Religion often plays a central role in Igbo culture, and for many Igbo men, passing on their faith and religious traditions is a key priority. Non-Igbo women, who may come from different religious backgrounds—or who may be less religious—must navigate these expectations while maintaining their own beliefs and values.

Successful negotiation of religious differences involves open communication about how religious practices will be integrated into family life, raising children with a sense of both traditions and creating new, shared rituals that honour both partners' faiths. Couples who find this balance often discover that their religious differences can enrich their marriage, providing opportunities for growth, understanding, and mutual respect.

Key strategies include respecting each other's religious practices, blending traditions where possible, and fostering an environment of tolerance and openness. By building a strong foundation of trust and communication, couples can navigate the complexities of religious differences while maintaining a unified and loving relationship.

Key Takeaway Lessons from Chapter 20

1. **Respecting Religious Practices**

    o   Understanding and respecting the role of religion in Igbo culture is essential for fostering harmony in cross-cultural marriages. Even if one partner does not share the same faith, respecting religious practices, such as attending church or participating in key celebrations, strengthens the relationship.

    o   **Lesson:** Respect for a partner's religious beliefs, even without full participation, demonstrates mutual understanding and strengthens marital bonds.

2. **Finding Balance Between Religious Practices**

    o   Navigating differing religious practices requires open communication and compromise. Couples can create harmony by blending traditions, attending key celebrations, or agreeing on separate practices without imposing beliefs on each other.

- o **Lesson**: Balancing religious practices allows both partners to honour their faiths while fostering unity in the marriage.

3. **Coordinating Religious Upbringing for Children**

- o Raising children with shared or dual religious traditions often requires negotiation. Couples might decide to raise children in one faith while exposing them to other traditions or take a secular approach emphasizing shared values.

- o **Lesson**: Coordinating a unified approach to religious upbringing ensures children appreciate and respect both parents' beliefs.

4. **Blending and Creating New Traditions**

- o Combining elements of both partners' religious traditions or creating new shared rituals fosters inclusivity and unity within the family. These practices help bridge differences and create a unique family culture.

- o **Lesson**: Blended traditions or new shared rituals strengthen family bonds and enrich the marriage by celebrating diversity.

5. **Fostering Mutual Respect and Tolerance**

- o Successful cross-cultural marriages thrive on mutual respect and tolerance for differing beliefs. Creating an inclusive environment where both partners feel valued helps build trust and strengthens the relationship.

o **Lesson**: Respect and tolerance for each other's beliefs transform religious differences into opportunities for deeper connection and understanding.

By embracing respect, communication, and compromise, couples can navigate religious differences while enriching their shared lives with the strength of faiths and traditions.

Chapter 21:
BUILDING A SHARED IDENTITY IN CROSS-CULTURAL MARRIAGES

Introduction

B uilding a shared identity in cross-cultural marriages can be one of the relationship's most enriching yet challenging aspects. For Igbo men married to non-Igbo women, this process involves blending distinct cultural, linguistic, and social traditions to create a unified identity that reflects both partners' backgrounds. Shared identity is about honouring the traditions each partner brings into the marriage and crafting new rituals, values, and practices that represent the couple's unique dynamic. Successful cross-cultural marriages often result in a strong, hybrid family culture that respects each partner's heritage while creating space for new shared experiences.

1. Embracing Both Cultures in Daily Life

For many couples in cross-cultural marriages, building a shared identity starts with embracing elements from both cultures in their daily lives. This might involve incorporating foods, languages, clothing, and customs from both partners' cultures into the household. Non-Igbo women often find that embracing Igbo culture—such as preparing traditional dishes or learning aspects of the language—can help create a sense of unity within the marriage.

Similarly, Igbo men who respect and incorporate their partner's cultural practices into family life help balance the two worlds.

Blending Everyday Practices

Incorporating elements of both cultures into daily life helps build a shared identity that celebrates the richness of each partner's background. This often starts with simple gestures, such as cooking meals from both cultures and blending parenting styles that reflect the values of both partners.

- **Participant 1 (Non-Igbo Woman, 31 years old, married for 5 years):**

"One way we've built a shared identity is by embracing each other's cultures in small, everyday ways. We cook traditional Igbo meals and have dishes from my culture. It's become a way to celebrate our backgrounds without losing what makes us unique."

- **Participant 2 (Igbo Man, 40 years old, married to a Dutch woman):**

"We've made it a point to honour our cultures at home. We speak English mostly, but I teach our children Igbo, and my wife introduces them to her language and traditions. It's created a balance where both cultures are respected."

2. Creating New Family Traditions

While honouring each partner's cultural heritage is important, couples in cross-cultural marriages often find that creating new family traditions is essential for building a shared identity. These new traditions may be a blend of both cultures, or they may be unique to the couple and their children. Establishing shared rituals around holidays, family meals, or annual events helps strengthen the family bond and creates continuity for future generations.

Blending or Inventing Traditions

Couples who successfully build a shared identity often blend important traditions from both cultures or invent new ones that are meaningful to their family. These new rituals help bring both partners together in a way that reflects their unique relationship, creating a new identity for their family.

- **Participant 3 (Non-Igbo Woman, 33 years old, married for 6 years):**

"We've blended some of our cultural traditions to create family rituals. For example, we celebrate Christmas in a way that honours both his religious traditions and my more secular approach. It's become a special time for us, and our kids are growing up with a mix of both cultures."

- **Participant 4 (Igbo Man, 38 years old, married to an American woman):**

"Creating our family traditions has helped us build a shared identity. We've kept some traditional Igbo practices, but we've also started new traditions that are meaningful to us as a couple. It's helped us create a sense of unity while respecting where we both come from."

3. Navigating Cultural Differences in Parenting

Parenting is often an area where cultural differences become most pronounced, and how couples navigate these differences plays a crucial role in building a shared identity. Igbo men may bring traditional parenting practices rooted in discipline, respect for elders, and strong family bonds. At the same time, non-Igbo women may have different views on raising children, especially when it comes to independence and decision-making. Blending these approaches helps create a parenting style that reflects both partners' values and strengthens the family's shared identity.

Creating a Unified Parenting Approach

By blending parenting practices from both cultures, couples can create a parenting style that reflects their shared values while honouring each partner's background. This requires open communication and a willingness to adapt, but it ultimately strengthens the family's identity by creating consistency for the children.

- **Participant 5 (Non-Igbo Woman, 35 years old, married for 8 years):**

"Parenting was one of the hardest areas for us to figure out. My husband has a more traditional approach, while I lean towards giving our kids more independence. We've learned to blend both styles, teaching them respect and discipline while encouraging them to make their own choices. It's helped us create a unified front as parents."

- **Participant 6 (Igbo Man, 41 years old, married to a Canadian woman):**

"Our parenting styles were very different because of our cultural backgrounds, but we've found a way to blend them over time. We emphasize respect and family values from my culture, but we've also adopted some of my wife's ideas about independence and creativity. It's created a parenting style that reflects both of us."

4. Language and Communication in Building Identity

Language plays a key role in shaping identity, and in cross-cultural marriages, it often serves as both a unifying and challenging factor. For Igbo men, teaching their children the Igbo language is a way of passing down cultural heritage, while non-Igbo women may introduce their native language as well. Finding a balance between languages helps create a bilingual or multilingual environment where both cultures are celebrated. The language used in communication within the family also impacts how children understand and connect with both sides of their heritage.

Creating a Bilingual or Multilingual Home

Building a shared identity in cross-cultural marriages often involves raising children to speak both languages, allowing them to connect with their parents' backgrounds. Couples prioritizing bilingualism or multilingualism create a family identity honouring both cultures.

- **Participant 7 (Non-Igbo Woman, 30 years old, married for 4 years):**

"We've made it a point to teach our children both English and Igbo. My husband speaks Igbo to them, and I speak English. It's important to both of us that they grow up knowing both sides of their heritage, and language is a big part of that."

- **Participant 8 (Igbo Man, 39 years old, married to a British woman):**

"Teaching our kids Igbo has been essential to me. It's not just about the language—it's about making sure they feel connected to their roots. My wife has been very supportive, and we've also introduced them to aspects of her culture. It's created a strong sense of identity for our family."

5. Celebrating Cultural Diversity in Social Circles

Building a shared identity does not happen only within the home—it also extends into the couple's social circles. For many cross-cultural couples, developing a diverse network of friends who embrace both cultures helps reinforce their shared identity. Whether attending cultural events, participating in community celebrations, or inviting friends from both backgrounds into their homes, having a supportive social circle that respects and celebrates the couple's diversity can strengthen their marriage.

Building a Diverse Social Network

By cultivating friendships and connections with people who respect and celebrate both partners' cultures, couples can build a broader sense of identity that extends beyond the family unit. This external support helps reinforce the couple's shared values and provides a strong foundation for their marriage.

- **Participant 9 (Non-Igbo Woman, 34 years old, married for 6 years):**

"We've tried to build a social circle that reflects our backgrounds. We have friends from my culture and his, and we all come together for different celebrations and events. It's been a great way to celebrate our diversity and create a shared identity that includes our friends and family."

- **Participant 10 (Igbo Man, 42 years old, married to a German woman):**

"Having friends who understand and respect our cultures has made a big difference. We attend Igbo community events and celebrate traditions from my wife's culture. It's helped us build a support system reinforcing our shared identity."

6. Building a Shared Identity Through Compromise

In any cross-cultural marriage, compromise is essential for building a shared identity. Partners must be willing to adapt, learn from each other, and find ways to blend their values and traditions. This give-and-take process helps strengthen the marriage by ensuring both partners feel respected and valued. The ability to compromise—whether about holiday celebrations, religious practices, or parenting styles—creates a foundation for a lasting and unified identity as a couple.

Finding Common Ground Through Compromise

For many couples, compromise is the key to building a shared identity. By making room for each other's values and traditions, couples can create a family culture that reflects their backgrounds while fostering a sense of unity.

- **Participant 11 (Non-Igbo Woman, 33 years old, married for 5 years):**

"We've had to compromise on many things, from how we celebrate holidays to how we raise our kids. It hasn't always been easy, but we've learned to respect each other's perspectives and find a middle ground. That's what's helped us build a shared identity."

- **Participant 12 (Igbo Man, "41 years old, married to an Italian   woman):**
  "Compromise has been essential for us. Sometimes, we've had to adapt to each other's traditions and ways of doing things. I've had to be flexible about certain cultural practices, and my wife has done the same. It's helped us create a unique family identity where both cultures are valued."

7. Passing Down a Blended Cultural Heritage to Children

- One of the most significant ways cross-cultural couples build a shared identity is through their children. Raising children in a multicultural environment presents an opportunity to pass down both parents' values, traditions, and languages. For Igbo men, instilling pride in Igbo culture, values, and traditions is often essential to raising children. At the same time, non-Igbo women want to ensure that their children are also connected to their cultural background. By blending these heritages, couples can give their children a wealthy, diverse upbringing, honouring both sides of their family.

Creating a Multicultural Upbringing for Children

- Couples who successfully blend their cultural heritage often do so by intentionally teaching their children about both sides of their family, whether through language, traditions, or cultural practices. Raising children proud of their multicultural background helps solidify a shared family identity.

- **Participant 13 (Non-Igbo Woman, 36 years old, married for 8 years):**

  "It's important to both of us that our kids understand both sides of their heritage. We've made it a priority to teach them about my culture and his, and they're growing up speaking both languages and participating in traditions from both backgrounds. It's something that has brought us together as a family."

- **Participant 14 (Igbo Man, 40 years old, married to a French woman):**

  "Raising children in a cross-cultural marriage has been one of the most rewarding parts of our relationship. We've taught them to embrace both sides of their identity, and they're growing up knowing where they come from. It's something that has made our family stronger."

8. Creating a Unified Family Vision

- Building a shared identity in cross-cultural marriages often involves creating a unified vision for the future that reflects the couple's shared goals, values, and aspirations. This vision may include how they want to raise their children, the kind of home they want to build, and the family traditions they want to establish. Couples can create a strong sense of unity and direction in their marriage by discussing their long-term goals and aligning their visions for the future.

Defining a Shared Future

- Couples who take the time to define their shared vision often find that it brings them closer together and gives them a sense of purpose. This shared vision may include elements from both cultures and new goals that reflect their unique partnership.

- **Participant 15 (Non-Igbo Woman, 32 years old, married for 6 years):**

  "We've spent much time discussing our future and what we want for our family. It's important to both of us that we raise our children with values from both cultures, but we've also created new goals that are ours. A shared vision has helped us stay united, even when things get challenging."

- **Participant 16 (Igbo Man, 39 years old, married to a German woman):**

  "Our shared vision has been key to building a strong family identity. We've talked about everything—from how we want to raise our kids to the legacy we want to leave behind. It's helped us create a sense of unity and purpose that goes beyond our cultural differences."

Building a shared identity in cross-cultural marriages between Igbo men and non-Igbo women involves blending distinct cultural traditions, values, and practices into a unified family dynamic. This process requires open communication, compromise, and a willingness to embrace each other's backgrounds while creating new traditions that reflect the couple's unique relationship. Through blending everyday practices, creating new family traditions, navigating cultural differences in parenting, and fostering a bilingual or multilingual environment, couples can build a family identity that honours both cultures.

Raising children with a strong sense of both parents' heritage while creating a unified vision for the family's future helps cross-cultural couples form a cohesive and lasting bond. Couples create an inclusive environment reinforcing their shared identity by embracing diversity within their marriage and social circles. Ultimately, the success of building a shared identity lies in mutual respect, compromise, and the commitment to creating a family culture that reflects the richness of both partners' backgrounds.

Key Takeaway Lessons from Chapter 21

1. **Embrace Both Cultures in Daily Life**

   o Incorporating elements from both partners' cultures into daily practices, such as food, language, and traditions, strengthens the marriage and creates a balanced home environment.

   o **Lesson**: Celebrating both cultures daily fosters mutual respect and builds a shared family identity.

2. **Create New Family Traditions**

   o Blending traditions from both cultures or inventing unique family rituals creates a strong bond and sense of unity. These traditions reflect the couple's shared values and provide continuity for future generations.

   o **Lesson**: Establishing new traditions helps couples build a family culture that respects their diverse backgrounds while creating something uniquely theirs.

3. Blend Parenting Styles

o Parenting often highlights cultural differences, but couples can create a unified approach by blending practices from both traditions. This balance teaches children respect for both cultures while establishing shared family values.

o **Lesson:** Collaborative parenting that blends cultural influences strengthens family identity and supports children's holistic development.

4. Foster a Multilingual and Multicultural Environment

o Language is a key component of cultural heritage. Raising bilingual or multilingual children helps preserve both parents' identities while fostering an appreciation for diversity.

o **Lesson:** Emphasizing bilingualism or multilingualism connects children to both cultures, reinforcing a shared family identity.

5. Build a Unified Vision for the Future

o Defining shared goals and aspirations strengthens the marriage and provides a sense of direction for the family. This vision incorporates elements from both cultures and aligns with the couple's partnership.

o **Lesson:** Creating a shared vision for the future helps couples stay united and focused on building a lasting family legacy.

By blending cultural practices, creating new traditions, and fostering mutual respect, couples in cross-cultural marriages can build a shared identity that celebrates the richness of both partners' heritage.

Chapter 22:
DEALING WITH MISCONCEPTIONS ABOUT IGBO MEN IN CROSS-CULTURAL MARRIAGES

Introduction

In cross-cultural marriages involving Igbo men and non-Igbo women, various misconceptions can arise due to cultural differences and stereotypes. These misconceptions can range from assumptions about gender roles, personality traits, and financial habits to familial expectations. For non-Igbo women, navigating these misunderstandings is essential for building a strong, balanced relationship based on mutual respect and clear communication. Addressing these misconceptions can help both partners grow closer as they work to understand and appreciate each other's perspectives.

1. Misconception: Igbo Men Are Solely Focused on Wealth

One common stereotype about Igbo men is that they focus on wealth and financial success. This misconception often arises from the entrepreneurial nature of the Igbo people, who are known for their business acumen and drive for economic success. While it is true that many Igbo men place a strong emphasis on providing for their families, this does not mean that they prioritize wealth over love, family, or personal relationships.

Understanding the Cultural Value of Financial Stability

For many Igbo men, financial success is seen as a way to ensure the security and well-being of their family, which is a deeply held cultural value. Non-Igbo women may initially misinterpret this emphasis on financial stability as materialism, but understanding the cultural context can help shift this perception.

- **Participant 1 (Non-Igbo Woman, 34 years old, married for 6 years):**

"At first, I thought my husband was overly focused on making money. He always talked about his business and investments; I felt he put wealth above everything else. Nevertheless, over time, I realized that for him, providing for the family is a way of showing love. His focus on financial stability is rooted in wanting to care for us."

- **Participant 2 (Igbo Man, 39 years old, married to an American woman):**

"In Igbo culture, being a provider is a point of pride. It's not about materialism—it's about ensuring your family is taken care of. My wife wasn't used to this at first, but once we talked about it, she understood that my drive for financial success is about building a strong foundation for our future."

2. Misconception: Igbo Men Are Traditional and Domineering

Another common misconception is that Igbo men are overly traditional, especially when it comes to gender roles, and that they expect to dominate the household. This stereotype can be intimidating for non-Igbo women, especially those who come from cultures where gender equality is emphasized. While Igbo culture has traditionally assigned distinct roles to men and women, many Igbo men in cross-cultural marriages are open to more egalitarian relationships where responsibilities are shared.

Redefining Gender Roles in Cross-Cultural Marriages

Non-Igbo women may initially be concerned about traditional gender expectations, but many Igbo men are willing to redefine these roles, blending the strengths of both cultures. Couples can build partnerships based on equality and mutual respect by communicating openly about expectations.

- **Participant 3 (Non-Igbo Woman, 32 years old, married for 5 years):**

"I was worried that my husband would expect me to fulfill traditional gender roles, like taking care of the house while he worked. But once we discussed it, I realized he values equality in our relationship. We share responsibilities, and he respects my independence and career just as much as I respect his."

- **Participant 4 (Igbo Man, 41 years old, married to a French woman):**

"I grew up in a culture where men were expected to be the head of the household, but my wife and I have created a partnership that reflects our values. We share responsibilities, and I've learned to be more open to her gender-role perspective. It's helped us create a stronger, more balanced marriage."

3. Misconception: Igbo Men Are Not Emotionally Expressive

A common misconception about Igbo men is that they are emotionally reserved and do not openly express their feelings. This can sometimes create a barrier in cross-cultural marriages, where non-Igbo women may be more accustomed to frequent emotional expressions and verbal affirmations of love. While it's true that some Igbo men may be more reserved due to cultural expectations of masculinity, many are willing to learn new ways of expressing emotions and connecting with their partners.

Learning Emotional Expression Across Cultures

For non-Igbo women, understanding that emotional expression can take different forms in different cultures is key to overcoming this misconception. Igbo men often show their love and commitment through actions rather than words, but with time, many become more comfortable with verbal and emotional expression.

- **Participant 5 (Non-Igbo Woman, 30 years old, married for 4 years):**

"In the beginning, I felt like my husband wasn't as emotionally expressive as I was used to. He didn't often say 'I love you' and wasn't open about his feelings. But I soon realized that he shows his love through his actions—he's always there for me and works hard to care for our family. Over time, he's also become more comfortable expressing his emotions verbally."

- **Participant 6 (Igbo Man, 38 years old, married to a British woman):**

"In my culture, men aren't always taught to be emotionally expressive, but my wife helped me understand how important it is to share my feelings. I've learned to open up more, and it's made our relationship stronger. Now, I'm more comfortable expressing love in different ways."

4. Misconception: Igbo Men Are Dominated by Their Families

A common concern for non-Igbo women is the belief that Igbo men are overly influenced by their extended families, particularly their parents. In Igbo culture, family ties are significant, and decisions are often made in consultation with elders. This can be misinterpreted by non-Igbo women as a lack of independence. While family plays a significant role, many Igbo men in cross-cultural marriages work to balance honouring their family's expectations and prioritizing their spouse.

Balancing Family Expectations and Independence

Non-Igbo women may initially feel that their Igbo husband's family has too much influence over their relationship. However, many Igbo men strive to balance family obligations with their spouse's needs. Open communication about boundaries and expectations is crucial for maintaining harmony between the couple and the extended family.

- **Participant 7 (Non-Igbo Woman, 35 years old, married for 7 years):**

"I was worried that my husband's family would have too much influence over our decisions, especially since they're so close. But he's been great about setting boundaries and ensuring our marriage comes first. He respects his family but always puts our relationship at the center."

- **Participant 8 (Igbo Man, 40 years old, married to a Canadian woman):**

"Family is important in Igbo culture, but I've learned how to balance that with my marriage. My wife had concerns about how involved my family would be in our lives, but we've set boundaries that work for both of us. It's about respecting family while also protecting our relationship."

5. Misconception: Igbo Men Expect Traditional Marriages

Some non-Igbo women may worry that Igbo men expect their marriages to follow strictly traditional lines, with defined roles for men and women and rigid expectations around family life. However, many Igbo men, particularly those in cross-cultural marriages, are open to creating modern, flexible relationships that reflect their partner's values and beliefs. This flexibility allows for blending cultural traditions and contemporary relationship dynamics.

Creating a Modern Marriage

While traditional values are important, many Igbo men in cross-cultural marriages are open to adopting modern approaches, where responsibilities and roles are shared. This balance creates a marriage that reflects both partners' identities and values.

- **Participant 9 (Non-Igbo Woman, 29 years old, married for 5 years):**

"I was initially worried that my husband would expect a traditional marriage, where I would take on most domestic duties. But he's supported my career, and we share household responsibilities. We've built a marriage honouring our backgrounds and reflecting our modern values."

- **Participant 10 (Igbo Man, 39 years old, married to a Dutch woman):**

"I respect the traditions I grew up with, but my marriage differs from my parents'. We've created our version of marriage that works for us, blending traditional values with modern approaches. It's allowed us to respect our cultures while building a strong, equal partnership."

Summary

In cross-cultural marriages involving Igbo men and non-Igbo women, dealing with **misconceptions** about Igbo men is an essential step toward building a strong, healthy relationship. Misunderstandings about Igbo men being overly focused on wealth, traditional gender roles, emotional expression, family dominance, and traditional marriages can create barriers that prevent couples from fully understanding and appreciating each other. By openly communicating about these misconceptions and working to address cultural differences, couples can foster mutual respect and create relationships that blend the best aspects of both cultures.

Through compromise, learning, and understanding, couples can break down stereotypes and build a strong, unified relationship that reflects the uniqueness of their cross-cultural experience. Whether redefining gender roles, balancing family expectations, or finding new ways to express love and emotion, overcoming misconceptions allows both partners to grow closer and build a partnership based on equality, trust, and shared **values**. As couples navigate these cultural challenges, they often find that their relationship is enriched by blending traditions and perspectives, leading to a more fulfilling and dynamic partnership.

Key Takeaways from Chapter 22

1. **Cultural Context**: Many misconceptions about Igbo men stem from cultural misunderstandings. Financial focus, gender roles, emotional expression, and family involvement must be understood in the context of Igbo cultural values, prioritizing family, stability, and respect for tradition.

2. **Open Communication**: Addressing these misconceptions requires honest conversations about cultural expectations

and values. Couples who take the time to communicate and learn about each other's backgrounds can better overcome misunderstandings and build stronger relationships.

3. **Mutual Respect**: Non-Igbo women can help dispel stereotypes by approaching these cultural differences with curiosity and respect. Igbo men can work toward creating a balanced partnership that honours both partners' values.

4. **Blended Traditions**: Successful cross-cultural marriages involve blending traditional values with modern approaches. This balance allows couples to build relationships that respect both cultures while reflecting contemporary realities.

5. **Setting Boundaries**: In many cases, setting clear boundaries, particularly around family involvement, is essential for creating a harmonious relationship that prioritizes the couple's needs while respecting cultural norms.

Dealing with misconceptions about Igbo men in cross-cultural marriages requires **understanding, communication, and compromise**. By addressing common misunderstandings—such as those related to wealth, gender roles, emotional expression, family dynamics, and traditional values—couples can foster a deeper appreciation for one another's backgrounds and build a relationship based on trust, equality, and mutual respect. As non-Igbo women and their Igbo husbands navigate these cultural differences, they can create a strong, shared identity that blends the best of both worlds, enriching their marriage and strengthening their bond.

Chapter 23:
MANAGING CONFLICT IN CROSS-CULTURAL MARRIAGES

Managing Conflict in Cross-Cultural Marriages

onflict is a natural part of any relationship, but in cross-cultural marriages, it can be intensified by differences in cultural norms, communication styles, values, and expectations. In marriages between Igbo men and non-Igbo women, these cultural differences can create unique challenges that require thoughtful navigation. Managing conflict in cross-cultural marriages involves open communication, patience, and a willingness to learn and adapt. By understanding the root causes of conflict and finding strategies that honour both partners' backgrounds, couples can resolve disputes to strengthen their relationship rather than divide it.

1. Understanding Cultural Differences as a Source of Conflict

One of the primary sources of conflict in cross-cultural marriages is differences in cultural values and practices. For Igbo men and non-Igbo women, these differences might manifest in areas such as gender roles, family obligations, communication styles, and expectations around marriage. Recognizing that cultural norms shape each partner's perspective can help couples approach conflicts with greater empathy and understanding.

Acknowledging Cultural Differences in Conflict Resolution

Non-Igbo women and their Igbo husbands often find that their respective cultural backgrounds shape their approach to conflict. Understanding and acknowledging these differences as part of the conflict can help couples navigate disputes more effectively.

- **Participant 1 (Non-Igbo Woman, 31 years old, married for 5 years):**

"At first, I didn't realize how much of our disagreements were rooted in cultural differences. We approached things like family obligations and decision-making differently, leading to misunderstandings. Once we started recognizing that our backgrounds influenced how we dealt with conflict, it became easier to find common ground."

- **Participant 2 (Igbo Man, 40 years old, married to a British woman):**

"Growing up, I was taught to handle conflict in a certain way—by staying calm and not being overly emotional. On the other hand, my wife is more open about expressing her feelings. It took time for us to understand each other's approaches, but now we try to find a middle ground."

2. Communication Styles and Conflict Resolution

Communication plays a critical role in conflict resolution, and in cross-cultural marriages, differences in communication styles can escalate or de-escalate conflicts. Igbo men may be more reserved in expressing emotions or conflict, preferring to maintain calm and composure. At the same time, non-Igbo women, particularly those from Western cultures, may value direct and open communication.

Finding a balance between these styles is essential for resolving conflicts without letting them spiral into more significant issues.

Adapting Communication Styles

Couples in cross-cultural marriages must adapt their communication styles to accommodate each other's needs. This may involve one partner learning to express their emotions more openly while the other practices patience and listening. Open and honest dialogue is key to resolving conflicts constructively.

- **Participant 3 (Non-Igbo Woman, 34 years old, married for 6 years):**

"I'm used to being very direct regarding conflict, but my husband tends to be more reserved. I would get frustrated early on because he wasn't addressing issues head-on. Over time, I've learned to be more patient, and he's become more comfortable sharing his feelings. We've found a balance that works for us."

- **Participant 4 (Igbo Man, 38 years old, married to a Canadian woman):**

"In my culture, we don't always express emotions openly during conflict. It was different for my wife, who's very open about her feelings. We had to learn how to communicate in a way that worked for both of us. Now, we've developed a way to talk through problems without escalating them."

3. Family Involvement as a Source of Conflict

In Igbo culture, extended family plays a significant role in personal life, and family members may often have a say in important decisions. For non-Igbo women, this level of family involvement can sometimes feel intrusive, especially if they come from cultures where individual decision-making is emphasized. This dynamic can lead to conflict if boundaries around family involvement are not established.

Setting Boundaries Around Family Involvement

Navigating family dynamics requires clear communication and boundary-setting. Couples need to discuss how much involvement from extended family is appropriate and find a compromise that respects cultural values while maintaining the integrity of the marriage.

- **Participant 5 (Non-Igbo Woman, 33 years old, married for 4 years):**

"Initially, I found it hard to adjust to how involved my husband's family was in our life. I wasn't used to making decisions as a group, and it felt overwhelming. We had to have a lot of conversations about setting boundaries, and now we've found a way to respect his family's input without letting it interfere with our relationship."

- **Participant 6 (Igbo Man, 39 years old, married to a Dutch woman):**

"My wife wasn't used to our close family ties in Igbo culture, which led to some tension. We've worked out a system where we respect my family's role but also ensure that our marriage comes first. Setting boundaries has helped us avoid conflicts that come from family involvement."

4. Conflict Over Gender Roles and Expectations

Differences in expectations around gender roles can be another significant source of conflict in cross-cultural marriages. In traditional Igbo culture, men are expected to be the providers and heads of the household, while women are seen as nurturers and caretakers. Non-Igbo women, particularly those from cultures that emphasize gender equality, may struggle with these expectations, leading to tension over how responsibilities should be divided.

Negotiating Gender Roles

In cross-cultural marriages, couples must negotiate gender roles that reflect their cultural backgrounds and personal beliefs. Finding a balance between traditional and modern gender expectations can help reduce conflict and create a more equitable partnership.

- **Participant 7 (Non-Igbo Woman, 32 years old, married for 5 years):**

"There were times when I felt like my husband expected me to take on traditional gender roles, like handling all the housework. But we talked about it, and now we share responsibilities. It wasn't always easy, but it's helped us avoid conflict over who does what in the relationship."

- **Participant 8 (Igbo Man, 40 years old, married to an American woman):**

"In my culture, men are expected to be the providers, but I've learned that in our marriage, sharing responsibilities makes things work better. We've had to adjust our expectations of each other and find a balance that works for us."

5. Religious Differences and Conflict

For couples in cross-cultural marriages, religious differences can be a significant source of conflict, mainly if one partner is more religious than the other. Igbo men often have strong ties to their faith, which may be Christianity or traditional Igbo beliefs. At the same time, non-Igbo women may come from different religious backgrounds or be less religious. Disagreements about religious practices, especially when raising children, can lead to tension.

Respecting Religious Beliefs

Couples who successfully navigate religious differences do so by respecting each other's beliefs and finding common ground. This may involve participating in each other's religious practices or agreeing to incorporate both faiths into family life, particularly when raising children.

- **Participant 9 (Non-Igbo Woman, 35 years old, married for 7 years):**

"We come from different religious backgrounds, which caused conflict regarding how we wanted to raise our kids. We've found a way to respect our beliefs and ensure our children are exposed to both faiths. It's not always easy, but it's brought us closer together."

- **Participant 10 (Igbo Man, 42 years old, married to a French woman):**

"Religion was a source of conflict initially, especially since I'm more religious than my wife. We had to find a way to respect each other's beliefs without letting it cause tension. We've created a balance where we both feel comfortable with our religious practices."

6. Financial Disagreements and Cultural Expectations

Financial management is often a source of conflict in marriages, and in cross-cultural marriages, this can be amplified by different cultural expectations around money. In Igbo culture, men are expected to be the primary providers, and financial success is seen as a sign of stability and responsibility. Non-Igbo women may come from cultures where financial responsibilities are shared more equally, leading to spending, saving, and budgeting disagreements.

Compromising on Financial Management

Couples in cross-cultural marriages must compromise on managing their finances, balancing traditional expectations with modern financial practices. Open communication about financial goals and responsibilities is key to avoiding conflict.

- **Participant 11 (Non-Igbo Woman, 29 years old, married for 4 years):**

"We had a lot of disagreements about money at first. I'm used to managing my finances, and he felt responsible for providing for us. We've since found a system where we both contribute, but he still takes the lead in financial decisions. It's helped reduce conflict around money."

- **Participant 12 (Igbo Man, 38 years old, married to a British woman):**

"In my culture, men are expected to provide for the family, but I've learned that sharing financial responsibilities works better in our marriage. We've had to compromise on managing our money, and now we make financial decisions together."

Key Takeaways:

1. **Cultural Awareness**: Recognizing that cultural differences shape how conflicts are approached is essential for resolving disputes. Both partners must be aware of their cultural influences and how they affect their behaviour in conflict situations.

2. **Communication is Key**: Open, honest communication is critical for resolving conflict in cross-cultural marriages. Understanding each other's communication styles and adjusting accordingly can help avoid misunderstandings and build stronger connections.

3. **Compromise and Adaptability**: Flexibility and compromise are necessary when navigating differences in family expectations, gender roles, and financial management. Couples must be willing to adapt to each other's needs while finding solutions that work for both.

4. **Setting Boundaries**: Clear boundaries around family involvement are crucial for managing conflict and ensuring the couple's relationship remains the priority.

5. **Shared Values**: Despite cultural differences, couples can focus on shared values such as love, respect, and commitment to guide them through conflicts. This common ground can be the foundation for navigating even the most challenging disputes.

Managing conflict in cross-cultural marriages between Igbo men and non-Igbo women requires empathy, compromise, and open communication. Couples who approach conflict with an understanding of their cultural differences are better equipped to navigate disputes in a way that strengthens their relationship. By finding common ground, adapting communication styles, setting boundaries, and embracing compromise, couples can turn conflict into an opportunity for growth and deeper understanding.

Building a strong cross-cultural marriage is not about erasing differences but learning how to harmonize them. It is about creating a partnership honouring both partners' backgrounds while fostering a healthy, supportive, and loving relationship.

Chapter 24:

INTEGRATING IGBO CULTURAL VALUES IN CHILD-REARING

Introduction

Raising children in cross-cultural marriages can be both challenging and rewarding, mainly when parents are from different cultural backgrounds. For Igbo men married to non-Igbo women, integrating Igbo cultural values into child-rearing is often an important priority. The Igbo culture emphasizes values such as respect for elders, hard work, community, education, and strong family ties, all crucial in shaping a child's upbringing. For non-Igbo women, understanding these values and finding ways to incorporate them into a shared parenting approach can create a rich and diverse family environment. Couples can raise children proud of their multicultural heritage by blending parenting practices from both cultures.

1. Respect for Elders and Authority

In Igbo culture, respect for elders is a foundational value instilled in children from a young age. Elders are considered sources of wisdom and guidance; children are expected to show deference through actions and words. For non-Igbo women, this may be a different approach from what they are accustomed to, mainly if they come from cultures where independence and equality in relationships are emphasized.

Teaching Respect for Elders

Integrating this value into child-rearing requires teaching children to understand and appreciate the role of elders in the family and community. This may involve encouraging children to greet elders respectfully, listen to their advice, and follow cultural protocols that reflect this respect.

- **Participant 1 (Non-Igbo Woman, 32 years old, married for 6 years):**

"My husband places a lot of emphasis on our kids respecting their elders, which was different from how I grew up. At first, I didn't fully understand its cultural importance, but now I see how it helps our children stay connected to their roots. We've found a way to teach them respect for our families' traditions."

- **Participant 2 (Igbo Man, 38 years old, married to a Dutch woman):**

"In our culture, respect for elders is non-negotiable. I want my children to grow up with that same sense of respect, even though we live in a different cultural environment. My wife and I have found ways to incorporate this value into our parenting, and it's become a natural part of our family life."

2. Emphasis on Education and Hard Work

Education and hard work are core values in Igbo culture, where academic success is often seen as a pathway to personal and family advancement. Igbo families strongly emphasize education to achieve success and contribute to the community. For non-Igbo women, who may also value education, integrating this cultural aspect may require understanding the depth of this expectation and how it influences parenting decisions.

Promoting Education and Hard Work

Incorporating this Igbo value into child-rearing involves fostering a strong work ethic in children, encouraging them to take education seriously, and teaching them the importance of perseverance and discipline. This can be done through setting high academic expectations, supporting extracurricular activities that promote learning, and celebrating educational achievements.

- **Participant 3 (Non-Igbo Woman, 35 years old, married for 7 years):**

"Education is a big deal in our household, especially because it's an important part of my husband's culture. We make sure our kids understand the value of hard work and doing well in school, but we also balance it with letting them enjoy their childhood. It's been a great way to blend our values."

- **Participant 4 (Igbo Man, 40 years old, married to a Canadian woman):**

"In Igbo culture, education is key to success, and I want my children to have that same drive. My wife and I have worked together to ensure that our kids understand the importance of education and that they don't feel pressured. It's about creating a balance that reflects both our cultures."

3. The Importance of Family and Community

Igbo culture places a strong emphasis on family unity and community involvement. Children are taught from a young age that they are part of a larger family structure and that their actions reflect on themselves and their entire family. This collective mindset may require adjustment for non-Igbo women, who may come from more individualistic cultures, significantly when raising children within a more extensive family network.

Building Family and Community Ties

Incorporating this value into child-rearing involves teaching children about the importance of family connections, participating in family and community events, and fostering a sense of belonging. This can be achieved by encouraging children to spend time with extended family members, participate in cultural or religious ceremonies, and contribute to community initiatives.

- **Participant 5 (Non-Igbo Woman, 30 years old, married for 5 years):**

"My husband's family is very close-knit, and it's been important for him to pass that sense of community on to our kids. We ensure our children spend time with their extended family and learn about their cultural roots. It's been an adjustment for me, but I see how much our kids benefit from such a strong family sense."

- **Participant 6 (Igbo Man, 42 years old, married to an American woman):**

"In our culture, family is everything. I want my children to understand they are part of something bigger than themselves. My wife has embraced this, and we've worked together to ensure our kids know their relatives and participate in cultural events. It's helped them feel connected to both sides of their heritage."

4. Fostering a Sense of Responsibility

Igbo culture encourages children to take on responsibilities from a young age, whether helping around the house, contributing to the family's well-being, or participating in community activities. This sense of responsibility helps children develop discipline, accountability, and a strong work ethic. For non-Igbo women, fostering this value may require encouraging their children to take on more household or family responsibilities than they might be used to.

Encouraging Responsibility in Children

Incorporating this value involves teaching children to take responsibility for their actions, contribute to family chores, and develop a sense of accountability. This can be done through assigning age-appropriate tasks, encouraging children to contribute to family decisions, and teaching them the value of hard work and self-discipline.

- **Participant 7 (Non-Igbo Woman, 33 years old, married for 6 years):**

"We make sure our kids understand that they have responsibilities in the family, whether it's helping with chores or being respectful to others. It's been a great way to instill discipline and accountability, which are important values in my husband's culture."

- **Participant 8 (Igbo Man, 39 years old, married to a French woman):**

"In Igbo culture, children are expected to contribute to the household. My wife and I have ensured that our kids learn this early on by giving them responsibilities around the house. It's taught them the value of hard work and accountability, which is important in both cultures."

5. Religious and Spiritual Upbringing

Religion plays a significant role in Igbo culture, with many families strongly emphasizing religious teachings, practices, and spirituality. Religious values are often passed down to children through Christianity or traditional beliefs to instill moral guidance and a sense of purpose. For non-Igbo women, integrating these religious values into their parenting approach may require navigating their own religious beliefs or practices while ensuring that their children are exposed to their Igbo father's faith.

Integrating Religious Values

Incorporating religious values into child-rearing may involve regular participation in religious activities, teaching children about their spiritual heritage, and encouraging them to develop a personal sense of faith. Couples can work together to find ways to incorporate both religious traditions into their children's upbringing, fostering a spiritual identity that reflects both cultures.

- **Participant 9 (Non-Igbo Woman, 34 years old, married for 6 years):**

"Religion is important to my husband, and we've prioritized raising our children with those same values. We attend church together as a family, and I've learned much about his spiritual beliefs. It's been a great way to bond as a family while instilling moral values in our children."

- **Participant 10 (Igbo Man, 40 years old, married to a British woman):**

"Religion is a big part of Igbo culture, and I want my children to grow up with a strong sense of faith. My wife has been supportive, and we've found a way to integrate both of our spiritual beliefs into how we raise our kids. It's helped create a balanced spiritual upbringing for them."

Key Takeaways:

1. **Respect for Elders**: Teaching children to respect their elders is a key cultural value in Igbo culture. Non-Igbo women can support this value by encouraging respectful behaviour toward their family and their husband's extended family.

2. **Education and Hard Work**: Education is highly valued in Igbo culture as a path to success and self-advancement.

Parents can blend this cultural emphasis with their values, helping children develop a strong work ethic while balancing the pressures of academic achievement.

3. **Family and Community**: Fostering a strong sense of family and community ties is central to the Igbo way of life. Encouraging children to spend time with extended family, participate in cultural events, and understand the value of community helps build a strong sense of identity.

4. **Responsibility**: Igbo culture emphasizes integrating a sense of responsibility into child-rearing, which teaches children accountability, discipline, and the importance of contributing to the family's well-being.

5. **Religious and Moral Values**: Religious beliefs are an essential aspect of Igbo culture, and integrating these values into child-rearing ensures children develop a strong moral foundation. Blending both parents' spiritual traditions gives children a balanced and holistic approach to their faith.

Integrating Igbo cultural values into child-rearing in cross-cultural marriages between Igbo men and non-Igbo women provides children with a wealthy, diverse upbringing honouring both parents' heritage. Parents can create a well-rounded and culturally aware environment for their children by fostering respect for elders, emphasizing education and hard work, nurturing strong family and community bonds, promoting responsibility, and instilling religious and spiritual values.

Integrating these values involves communication, mutual respect, and a willingness to learn and adapt. By working together, couples can raise children proud of their multicultural heritage and equipped with the tools to navigate their Igbo roots and the broader world.

Chapter 25:

THE ROLE OF ELDERS AND ANCESTRAL LEGACY IN IGBO MARRIAGES

Introduction

In Igbo culture, the role of elders and the concept of ancestral legacy are deeply significant, particularly within the institution of marriage. Elders are considered custodians of tradition, wisdom, and family continuity, while ancestral legacy encompasses past generations' heritage. For Igbo men in cross-cultural marriages with non-Igbo women, understanding and integrating the influence of elders and the ancestral legacy into their relationships is vital. This cultural dynamic can shape how marriages function, the spouses' roles, and the expectations the wider family and community place upon the couple.

1. The Role of Elders in Guiding Marital Decisions

In Igbo culture, elders hold a position of high authority and respect, and they often serve as advisers and mediators in family matters, including marriage. Elders, whether parents, uncles, or other senior members of the family, are expected to provide wisdom and guidance to younger couples, particularly during important life events such as marriage. Their role is to ensure that traditional values are upheld and that the union aligns with the expectations of the family and the community.

Elders as Advisers and Mediators

For non-Igbo women, elders' involvement in marital decisions may seem overwhelming or intrusive at times, especially if they come from cultures where marriage is viewed more as a private matter between the couple. However, understanding the cultural significance of elders' involvement can help ease this tension and foster respect for their role in family life.

- **Participant 1 (Non-Igbo Woman, 34 years old, married for 7 years):**

"When we first married, I was surprised by how much my husband's parents and other elders were involved in decisions that I thought were just between us. It felt like there were so many people weighing in on our choices. But over time, I've understood that it's part of their culture. Elders are considered guardians of family traditions; their advice is meant to guide, not control."

- **Participant 2 (Igbo Man, 38 years old, married to a Canadian woman):**

"In my family, we turn to the elders for advice, especially on important matters like marriage. It's part of our tradition. My wife wasn't used to this, but we've learned to balance their input with our decisions. It's about respecting their role while establishing our boundaries as a couple."

2. Respecting Elders in Daily Marital Life

Respect for elders is not limited to formal occasions or family gatherings in Igbo culture—it extends to everyday life and interactions within the marriage. Elders are honoured through gestures such as greetings, care, and inclusion in family events. This respect reflects one's upbringing and values, strengthening the bonds between the couple and the extended family.

Integrating Respect for Elders into Marital Life

For non-Igbo women, learning to respect their Igbo husband's elders is essential for building a harmonious relationship with the extended family. This might include learning cultural customs, such as the appropriate way to greet elders or involve them in significant family decisions.

- **Participant 3 (Non-Igbo Woman, 30 years old, married for 5 years):**

"I wasn't used to the idea of greeting and interacting with elders in such a formal way. But I've come to appreciate how important it is in my husband's culture. I've learned how to show respect to his parents and the older members of the family, and it's strengthened my relationship with them."

- **Participant 4 (Igbo Man, 40 years old, married to an American woman):**

"Respect for elders is something we grow up with, and my wife and I must teach our children the same values. We've ensured they understand how to interact with their grandparents and the older community members, and my wife has embraced that as well."

3. Ancestral Legacy and Its Influence on Marriage

Ancestral legacy in Igbo culture is the idea that one's ancestors have a continuing presence and influence on the living. This legacy is honoured through rituals, stories, and family traditions passed down from generation to generation. For Igbo men, maintaining this ancestral connection is a way of preserving their heritage, which plays a vital role in marriage. Couples are expected to honour their ancestors, uphold family traditions, and pass these values on to their children.

Honouring Ancestral Legacy in Marriage

In cross-cultural marriages, incorporating the concept of ancestral legacy can be challenging but also enriching. Non-Igbo women may find it meaningful to learn about their husband's family history and participate in traditions honouring their ancestors, creating a bridge between the past and the future.

- **Participant 5 (Non-Igbo Woman, 32 years old, married for 6 years):**

"At first, I didn't fully understand the importance of the ancestral legacy in my husband's culture. However, as I learned more about his family's history and the stories passed down from his elders, I started to see how important it is to him. We now ensure that we honour those traditions in our family, and it's become something that connects us to his roots."

- **Participant 6 (Igbo Man, 39 years old, married to a Dutch woman):**

"Ancestral legacy is a big part of Igbo culture, which I want my children to understand. My wife has been supportive in learning about our family's history and the traditions we keep alive. We've made it a point to pass these stories and values on to our kids so they understand both sides of their heritage."

4. Elders' Role in Conflict Resolution

Elders in Igbo culture also play an essential role in resolving conflicts within marriages. When disputes arise between a couple, elders may step in to offer advice or mediate discussions to ensure that the marriage remains strong and harmonious. Their role as mediators is seen as a way to preserve the family structure and prevent issues from escalating.

Turning to Elders for Conflict Resolution

For non-Igbo women, the involvement of elders in resolving marital conflicts might be unfamiliar or uncomfortable, mainly if they are used to resolving issues privately. However, recognizing elders' wisdom and experience in conflict resolution can help couples benefit from this cultural practice.

- **Participant 7 (Non-Igbo Woman, 35 years old, married for 7 years):**

"There were times when my husband wanted to involve his parents or other elders in resolving conflicts, and I found it strange initially. I wasn't used to bringing family into our issues. But I've seen that their involvement isn't about controlling our relationship but offering guidance and keeping the family united."

- **Participant 8 (Igbo Man, 41 years old, married to a French woman):**

"In my culture, elders are often called on to help resolve conflicts in marriage. It's something that has been done for generations. My wife wasn't used to this initially, but we've learned to accept their guidance when necessary while ensuring we handle things privately when appropriate."

5. Preserving Family Lineage Through Marriage

In Igbo culture, marriage continues the family lineage and preserves the ancestral legacy. Elders often emphasize the importance of producing children who carry on the family name and uphold the values passed down through generations. This focus on lineage can sometimes create pressure for couples, particularly in cross-cultural marriages where views on family size and child-rearing may differ.

Balancing Family Legacy and Personal Choice

Couples in cross-cultural marriages may need to navigate the expectations placed on them by elders regarding family size and the continuation of the family name. It is crucial to balance respecting these cultural expectations and making decisions that reflect their values.

- **Participant 9 (Non-Igbo Woman, 33 years old, married for 5 years):**

"There was a lot of pressure from my husband's family to have children early in our marriage, and I wasn't prepared for that. It took some time for us to explain our plans and come to an agreement that respected our wishes and his family's expectations. Ultimately, we've found a balance that works for us."

- **Participant 10 (Igbo Man, 40 years old, married to a British woman):**

"In Igbo culture, continuing the family name is very important, and there's much emphasis on having children. My wife and I had to discuss this early on in our marriage, and we've found a way to respect both cultures while making the right decisions for us as a couple."

Key Takeaways from Chapter 25

1. **Elders as Custodians of Tradition:** Elders play a significant role in advising younger generations and ensuring family traditions are upheld in marriage. Non-Igbo women can learn to appreciate this guidance while balancing respecting elders and establishing their marital boundaries.

2. **Respect for Elders in Daily Life:** Showing respect to elders in everyday life is integral to Igbo culture. For non-Igbo women, learning and adopting these practices, such as formal

greetings and including elders in family decisions, helps strengthen familial bonds and fosters unity.

3. **Honouring Ancestral Legacy**: Ancestral legacy is a key aspect of Igbo family life, passed down through stories, rituals, and traditions. Integrating these elements into a cross-cultural marriage allows both partners to maintain a connection to the past while building a future together.

4. **Elders' Role in Conflict Resolution**: Elders often mediate conflicts and offer wisdom in Igbo marriages. While this may be unfamiliar to non-Igbo women, embracing this practice can offer valuable perspectives and help resolve disputes while preserving family unity.

5. **Family Lineage and Legacy**: Preserving family lineage through marriage and having children to continue the family name is a strong cultural expectation. Couples in cross-cultural marriages must navigate these pressures while balancing their personal choices and cultural values.

In **Igbo marriages**, the role of elders and ancestral legacy are deeply woven into the fabric of family life. Elders serve as respected advisers, guiding couples through important decisions and helping them resolve conflicts, while ancestral legacy connects the present to the past, reinforcing cultural values and family heritage. For non-Igbo women in cross-cultural marriages, embracing these cultural elements can be both a challenge and an opportunity to build deeper relationships with their husbands' families and strengthen the foundation of their marriage.

By understanding and respecting the influence of elders and the importance of ancestral legacy, couples can create a harmonious marriage that honours their Igbo heritage and the unique blend of cultures they bring into their family. Through communication, mutual respect, and a willingness to learn, couples can navigate these cultural dynamics and build a lasting partnership that reflects both the past and the future.

Chapter 26:

ADDRESSING FINANCIAL EXPECTATIONS AND RESPONSIBILITY IN CROSS-CULTURAL MARRIAGES

Introduction

Financial management is critical to any marriage, but financial expectations and responsibilities can become particularly complex in cross-cultural marriages. In Igbo culture, financial responsibility is often seen as a fundamental aspect of marriage, with strong expectations placed on men as the primary providers for their families. Non-Igbo women may come from cultures where financial responsibilities are shared more equally between partners, or financial independence is emphasized for both spouses. These differences can lead to misunderstandings and tension if not addressed early in the relationship. By exploring financial expectations openly and developing a shared financial approach, couples can navigate these challenges and build a stable, successful partnership.

1. Traditional Financial Roles in Igbo Marriages

In traditional Igbo culture, men are expected to be the primary breadwinner, responsible for providing for the family's financial needs. This includes supporting the immediate family and, in many cases, providing for extended family members. The concept of "family" in Igbo culture often extends beyond the nuclear unit. Men may feel obligated to contribute to the well-being of their parents, siblings, and other relatives. This sense of responsibility is deeply ingrained in the Igbo social structure and is considered a mark of success and honour.

Understanding Traditional Financial Expectations

This traditional financial expectation may be unfamiliar for non-Igbo women, especially if they come from cultures where financial responsibilities are more equally divided between spouses. Understanding the cultural significance of financial provision in Igbo marriages is key to avoiding misunderstandings and establishing mutual respect.

- **Participant 1 (Non-Igbo Woman, 32 years old, married for 6 years):**

"In my culture, finances are usually shared equally between spouses, so when my husband insisted on taking care of most of the bills, I found adjusting hard. Nevertheless, I've come to understand that, for him, providing financially is part of his role as the head of the family. It's something he takes pride in."

- **Participant 2 (Igbo Man, 40 years old, married to a Canadian woman):**

"In our culture, men are expected to provide for their families. It's not just about money—it's about being responsible for the family's well-being. My wife wasn't used to this at first, but we've talked about it, and now we've found a balance where I still take the lead, but she also contributes."

2. Shared Financial Responsibilities in Cross-Cultural Marriages

While many Igbo men are obligated to be the primary providers, non-Igbo women may have different expectations about managing finances in a marriage. In many Western cultures, for example, financial independence for both partners is highly valued, and responsibilities such as paying bills, saving, and managing household expenses are often shared equally. Navigating these differences requires open communication and a willingness to adapt traditional roles to the realities of modern, cross-cultural relationships.

Finding Balance in Financial Responsibilities

For couples in cross-cultural marriages, finding a balance that respects both partners' values is essential. This might involve negotiating how household expenses are shared, savings and investments are managed, and financial decisions are made.

- **Participant 3 (Non-Igbo Woman, 34 years old, married for 7 years):**

"My husband initially wanted to handle all the financial responsibilities, but I was uncomfortable. I have always been financially independent, and I wanted to contribute. We have since found a system where we share the responsibilities. I handle certain expenses, and he takes care of others. It's a balance that works for us."

- **Participant 4 (Igbo Man, 38 years old, married to an American woman):**

"In my culture, men are expected to be the providers, but I've learned that in a cross-cultural marriage, sharing responsibilities can make things easier. My wife and I have divided the bills, which has taken some of the pressure off me. It's about finding what works for both partners."

3. Family Obligations and Financial Pressure

In Igbo culture, the expectation to provide for extended family members can place additional financial pressure on couples, particularly in cross-cultural marriages. Igbo men often feel a deep sense of responsibility to support their parents, siblings, and even more distant relatives, which can sometimes create tension if their non-Igbo spouse is not accustomed to this level of family obligation. Understanding the cultural importance of these obligations while setting boundaries to protect the financial health of the immediate family is critical.

Managing Family Obligations in Cross-Cultural Marriages

Non-Igbo women may need to learn about and respect the cultural expectations surrounding family obligations. In contrast, Igbo men may need to balance these obligations with the financial needs of their nuclear family. Open discussions about family support and setting clear financial boundaries can help manage these pressures.

- **Participant 5 (Non-Igbo Woman, 35 years old, married for 8 years):**

"I wasn't used to the idea of my husband sending money to his extended family regularly. In my culture, we usually prioritize our nuclear family first. It took some time to adjust, but I have learned to respect family's role in his culture. We have limits on how much we can contribute, so it doesn't affect our financial stability."

- **Participant 6 (Igbo Man, 39 years old, married to a French woman):**

"There is a strong expectation in our culture to take care of the extended family. My wife was not familiar with this, which caused some tension initially. However, we have found a way to balance it by setting aside a certain monthly amount for family support while ensuring we meet our financial goals."

4. Financial Transparency and Decision-Making

Financial transparency and joint decision-making are essential to successful financial management in cross-cultural marriages. In some cultures, each partner manages finances independently; in others, one partner may take the lead. In Igbo culture, the head of the household (traditionally the man) may make most of the financial decisions. However, in cross-cultural marriages, especially with non-Igbo women who may expect an equal say in financial matters, couples must establish a system where both partners are involved in financial planning and decision-making.

Building Financial Trust and Transparency

Open communication about finances, including income, expenses, savings, and long-term goals, is crucial for building trust and avoiding misunderstandings. Both partners should feel comfortable discussing money and making decisions together.

- **Participant 7 (Non-Igbo Woman, 30 years old, married for 5 years):**

"We've made it a priority to be completely transparent about our finances. We have regular discussions about our budget, savings, and plans. It was not something I was used to doing, but it's helped us avoid any major financial conflicts and keeps us on the same page."

- **Participant 8 (Igbo Man, 40 years old, married to a British woman):**

"In my culture, the man often makes the financial decisions, but my wife and I have agreed to make all major financial choices together.

We've learned to communicate openly about money, and it's brought us closer because we both feel involved in our financial future."

5. Cultural Expectations Around Wealth and Status

Igbo culture often sees wealth as a sign of success and social status. This can create additional pressure for Igbo men to achieve financial stability and success for their families and to meet societal expectations. Non-Igbo women may not be familiar with the cultural importance placed on wealth in Igbo society. They may prioritize other aspects of the marriage, such as emotional support or shared responsibilities. Understanding these cultural expectations can help couples manage financial pressures in a way that honours both partners' values.

Balancing Cultural Expectations and Personal Values

Couples in cross-cultural marriages must find a balance between the cultural emphasis on wealth and status and their values around financial success and well-being. This may involve redefining what success means for their family and ensuring financial decisions reflect both partners' priorities.

- **Participant 9 (Non-Igbo Woman, 33 years old, married for 5 years):**

"I wasn't used to the idea that wealth was so tied to status in my husband's culture. I come from a background where other things, like education and personal fulfillment, are more important. We have had to find a way to align our priorities, so we're not focused solely on financial success."

- **Participant 10 (Igbo Man, 38 years old, married to an American woman):**

"In Igbo culture, wealth is often seen as a measure of success, but I have learned that there are other ways to define success in our marriage. My wife and I have ensured that our financial goals reflect our cultural and personal values, so we are working towards a meaningful future for both of us."

Participant Quotes Recap:

- **Participant 1 (Non-Igbo Woman, 32 years old, married for 6 years):**

"I found it hard to adjust at first, but I've come to understand that for him, providing financially is part of his role as the head of the family. It's something he takes pride in."

- **Participant 3 (Non-Igbo Woman, 34 years old, married for 7 years):**

"We've found a system where we share the responsibilities. I handle certain expenses, and he takes care of others. It's a balance that works for us."

- **Participant 5 (Non-Igbo Woman, 35 years old, married for 8 years):**

"It took some time to adjust, but I've learned to respect the family's role in his culture. We've set limits on how much we can contribute, so it doesn't affect our financial stability."

- **Participant 7 (Non-Igbo Woman, 30 years old, married for 5 years):**

"We've made it a priority to be completely transparent about our finances. It's helped us avoid major financial conflicts and keeps us on the same page."

- **Participant 9 (Non-Igbo Woman, 33 years old, married for 5 years):**

"I wasn't used to the idea that wealth was so tied to status in my husband's culture. We've had to find a way to align our priorities, so we're not focused solely on financial success."

Key Takeaways from Chapter 26

1. **Understanding Traditional Roles**: In Igbo culture, men often feel responsible for providing for their families and extended family members. For non-Igbo women, understanding this cultural expectation is essential for navigating financial dynamics in the marriage.

2. **Balancing Responsibilities**: While traditional roles may suggest that men handle most financial responsibilities, cross-cultural marriages benefit from a balanced approach in which both partners contribute based on their strengths and preferences.

3. **Managing Family Obligations**: Financial support for extended family can create pressure, but couples can set boundaries and agree on a budget for family support to meet their nuclear family's needs.

4. **Financial Transparency**: Openness and honesty about finances, including income, expenses, and future goals, are essential for building trust and avoiding misunderstandings in cross-cultural marriages.

5. **Redefining Success**: In Igbo culture, wealth is often tied to status, but couples can redefine success to include personal values and shared goals that prioritize emotional well-being, stability, and fulfillment beyond financial gain.

Addressing financial expectations in cross-cultural marriages between Igbo men and non-Igbo women requires understanding, compromise, and open communication. While traditional Igbo values strongly emphasize financial provision and supporting extended family, non-Igbo women may come from cultures where financial independence and shared responsibilities are more common. Finding a balance between these perspectives involves mutual respect, clear communication about financial goals, and setting boundaries that protect the well-being of the immediate family while respecting cultural traditions.

Couples can foster a sense of unity, build trust, and ensure long-term financial stability by creating a shared financial strategy that reflects both partners' values and cultural backgrounds. Through transparency, compromise, and ongoing communication, cross-cultural marriages can successfully integrate financial expectations and create a strong foundation for their future.

Chapter 27:
CHALLENGES AND OPPORTUNITIES OF RAISING BICULTURAL CHILDREN

Introduction

R aising bicultural children presents both unique challenges and significant opportunities, particularly in cross-cultural marriages between Igbo men and non-Igbo women. Bicultural children grow up navigating two distinct cultural identities, often learning to balance the traditions, values, and expectations of both parents' backgrounds. In the context of Igbo culture, where community, family, and respect for traditions play a significant role, raising children who are connected to their Igbo roots while embracing the non-Igbo side of their heritage requires intentional parenting. While these children may face identity challenges, they also gain the opportunity to develop a broader worldview, greater adaptability, and a deep sense of cultural pride from both sides of their family.

1. Navigating Dual Cultural Expectations

One of the primary challenges of raising bicultural children is helping them navigate the dual expectations of their parents' distinct cultural backgrounds. In Igbo culture, strong emphasis is placed on respect for elders, community involvement, and family obligations. Non-Igbo cultures, particularly Western ones, may emphasize independence, individualism, and more relaxed family structures. These differing values can sometimes confuse children, who must learn to switch between cultural norms depending on the context.

Balancing Cultural Norms and Expectations

Parents in cross-cultural marriages must work together to balance the expectations of their respective cultures. For Igbo men and non-Igbo women, this may mean blending Igbo values of respect and community with the other parent's emphasis on individuality and independence, creating a supportive environment where children can thrive in both cultures.

- **Participant 1 (Non-Igbo Woman, 34 years old, married for 7 years):**

"Our kids are growing up with two very different sets of expectations—on one side, they're taught always to show respect for elders and family, while on the other, they're encouraged to express their opinions freely. It was confusing initially, but we've found a way to balance both sides, so they feel connected to both cultures."

- **Participant 2 (Igbo Man, 39 years old, married to a Canadian woman):**

"In Igbo culture, respect for elders and tradition is non-negotiable, but I've learned to appreciate my wife's culture's value on individuality. We've ensured our children understand both sides and learn when to follow each."

2. Language and Cultural Identity

Language is a central aspect of cultural identity, and for bicultural children, the challenge of mastering multiple languages can sometimes create confusion or frustration. For many Igbo men, passing down the Igbo language is a priority, as it connects to their cultural heritage and maintains family traditions. However, children may also need to become proficient in the language of their non-Igbo parent, creating a complex linguistic environment at home. Striking a balance between these languages while ensuring the child feels confident in both is integral to raising bicultural children.

Raising Bilingual or Multilingual Children

Encouraging children to learn both parents' languages requires consistent effort and support. While it may be challenging, raising bilingual or multilingual children allows them to navigate both cultures more easily and strengthens their connection to each side of their heritage.

- **Participant 3 (Non-Igbo Woman, 30 years old, married for 5 years):**

"Teaching our kids both Igbo and English has been challenging, especially since I don't speak Igbo fluently. But we've prioritized it, and now they're starting to pick up both languages. It's important to my husband that they can communicate with his family and stay connected to their Igbo roots."

- **Participant 4 (Igbo Man, 40 years old, married to a French woman):**

"I want my children to grow up speaking Igbo so they can stay connected to our culture, but I also know that being fluent in French and English will give them more opportunities. We've worked hard to ensure they're learning all three languages, and it has been worth the effort."

3. Negotiating Cultural Traditions and Celebrations

In cross-cultural marriages, blending traditions and celebrations from both cultures can create joyful opportunities and potential conflicts. For Igbo families, certain rituals and celebrations hold deep cultural significance, such as marriage ceremonies, naming ceremonies, and traditional holidays. Non-Igbo women may come from cultural backgrounds with different traditions and celebrations, leading to potential challenges in deciding how to integrate both customs into the children's lives.

Creating a Blended Tradition

Successfully raising bicultural children involves introducing them to the key traditions of both cultures and creating new family traditions that reflect both parents' backgrounds. This helps children feel a sense of belonging to both sides of their heritage while celebrating the richness of their diverse family history.

- **Participant 5 (Non-Igbo Woman, 35 years old, married for 6 years):**

"We've blended traditions from both cultures—our kids celebrate Christmas and Easter with my family, but they also participate in traditional Igbo ceremonies with their dad's side. It's been a beautiful way to expose them to both cultures and help them appreciate where they come from."

- **Participant 6 (Igbo Man, 38 years old, married to an American woman):**

"We make sure our kids celebrate important Igbo traditions, like the New Yam Festival, but we also respect my wife's cultural celebrations. We need to raise them with an understanding of both cultures so they do not feel like they have to choose between the two."

4. Dealing with Identity Confusion and Acceptance

One of the key challenges bicultural children face is navigating their sense of identity. Children growing up with two cultural backgrounds may sometimes feel conflicted about which culture they belong to, especially if they are surrounded by peers who identify with just one culture. Sometimes, they may experience external pressure to "choose" one identity over the other, leading to confusion or alienation.

Helping Children Build a Strong Sense of Identity

Parents in cross-cultural marriages must provide their children with the tools to build a strong bicultural identity that embraces both sides of their heritage. This involves fostering an environment where children feel comfortable exploring both cultures and teaching them to take pride in their unique backgrounds.

- **Participant 7 (Non-Igbo Woman, 33 years old, married for 5 years):**

"Our kids sometimes feel like they don't fully belong to either culture. We've tried to teach them that they don't have to choose— they're a mix of both cultures, and that's something to be proud of. It's not always easy, but we're helping them embrace both sides of their identity."

- **Participant 8 (Igbo Man, 40 years old, married to a British woman):**

"I grew up with a strong sense of my Igbo identity, and I want my children to have that too. However, I also understand that they're growing up in a different world, with influences from both sides of their family. We've made it a point to help them understand that being bicultural is a strength, not something to be confused about."

5. Opportunities for Broader Worldview and Adaptability

While raising bicultural children comes with challenges, it also provides significant opportunities for children to develop a broader worldview and greater adaptability. Growing up exposed to two cultures allows children to develop a deeper understanding of diversity, empathy, and adaptability in different social and cultural settings. This unique perspective can also help bicultural children excel in globalized environments, where being able to navigate multiple cultures is increasingly valuable.

Fostering a Global Perspective

Parents in cross-cultural marriages can capitalize on the opportunity to raise children who are comfortable navigating different cultural spaces. This may involve encouraging travel, participating in cultural events from both sides and teaching children about global diversity and the importance of empathy.

- **Participant 9 (Non-Igbo Woman, 30 years old, married for 6 years):**

"I love that our children are growing up exposed to both cultures. They're learning to appreciate diversity in a way that I didn't experience growing up, and I think it's making them more open-minded and adaptable."

- **Participant 10 (Igbo Man, 39 years old, married to a Dutch woman):**

"Raising bicultural children gives them a huge advantage in understanding different perspectives. They're growing up knowing how to navigate African and European cultures, which will help them socially and professionally."

Participant Quotes Recap:

- **Participant 1 (Non-Igbo Woman, 34 years old, married for 7 years):**

"Our kids are growing up with two very different sets of expectations… but we've found a way to balance both sides, so they feel connected to both cultures."

- **Participant 3 (Non-Igbo Woman, 30 years old, married for 5 years):**

"Teaching our kids both Igbo and English has been challenging, especially since I don't speak Igbo fluently. But we've prioritized it, and now they're starting to pick up both languages. It's important to my husband that they can communicate with his family and stay connected to their Igbo roots."

- **Participant 5 (Non-Igbo Woman, 35 years old, married for 6 years):**

"We've blended traditions from both cultures… Our kids celebrate Christmas and Easter with my family and participate in traditional Igbo ceremonies with their dad's side. It's been a beautiful way to expose them to both cultures."

- **Participant 7 (Non-Igbo Woman, 33 years old, married for 5 years):**

"Our kids sometimes feel like they don't fully belong to either culture. We've tried to teach them that they don't have to choose— they're a mix of both cultures, and that's something to be proud of."

- **Participant 9 (Non-Igbo Woman, 30 years old, married for 6 years):**

"I love that our children are growing up exposed to both cultures. They're learning to appreciate diversity in a way that I didn't experience growing up, and I think it's making them more open-minded and adaptable."

Key Takeaways from Chapter 27

1. **Dual Cultural Expectations**: Bicultural children may face the challenge of navigating different cultural expectations, such as balancing Igbo values of respect and family unity with other cultural norms of independence and individuality. Parents must create a supportive environment that honours both sets of expectations.

2. **Language as a Cultural Bridge**: Raising bilingual or multilingual children is challenging and rewarding. Parents should consistently reinforce both languages at home, helping children connect strongly to both cultural identities.

3. **Blending Traditions**: Cross-cultural families can create rich, diverse traditions by blending necessary customs from both cultures. This helps bicultural children feel connected to both sides of their heritage while enjoying unique family celebrations.

4. **Identity and Belonging**: Bicultural children may experience confusion about their identity. Parents must encourage them to embrace both sides of their cultural heritage and see their mixed identity as a source of strength and pride.

5. **Broader Worldview**: Raising bicultural children allows them to develop a global perspective and adaptability. Exposure to multiple cultures enhances their empathy, understanding, and ability to navigate diverse environments.

Raising **bicultural children** in cross-cultural marriages involves unique challenges, such as balancing dual cultural expectations, managing language acquisition, and helping children navigate their identity. At the same time, these challenges present significant opportunities for fostering a broader worldview, encouraging adaptability, and helping children take pride in their multicultural heritage.

Parents can ensure their children feel confident in both cultures by blending traditions, promoting bilingualism, and providing emotional support around identity. Ultimately, the experience of raising bicultural children enriches the family dynamic, allowing them to thrive in a multicultural world that values diversity and global understanding.

Figure 7: An Igbo Man, His Latino Wife and Two Bi-Racial Kids

EPILOGUE

Understanding each other's traditions, values, and expectations is key to building a harmonious and lasting relationship in cross-cultural marriages, where diverse cultural backgrounds converge to form a unique family unit. This research report has explored the complexities and beauty of cross-cultural marriages between Igbo men and non-Igbo women, highlighting various challenges and opportunities that arise from these unions. By navigating cultural expectations around marriage, family roles, financial responsibilities, child-rearing, and the influence of elders and ancestral legacy, couples can create meaningful partnerships rooted in respect, communication, and mutual understanding.

While each marriage is unique, the insights provided in this report aim to offer a comprehensive understanding of the factors that influence cross-cultural marriages involving Igbo men. However, it is essential to remember that this information is not meant to serve as a one-size-fits-all counsel for entering such relationships. Individuals and couples must approach their relationship with care, conducting necessary research and consultations to make informed decisions prioritizing their well-being.

1. Navigating Cultural Expectations in Marriage

At the heart of any successful cross-cultural marriage lies a deep respect for each other's culture. For Igbo men and non-Igbo women, this often means navigating dual expectations around gender roles, family involvement, and marital responsibilities. Igbo culture emphasizes respect for elders, strong family ties, and the role of men as providers. These values sometimes clash with other cultures' more egalitarian or individualistic norms.

Couples who successfully bridge these gaps do so through open communication and compromise. By finding a balance between traditional gender roles and modern expectations, setting boundaries around family involvement, and respecting each partner's contribution to the marriage, couples can create a partnership that honours both cultures. Non-Igbo women, for example, can learn to appreciate the wisdom and guidance of Igbo elders while asserting their independence and involvement in family decisions. This balance helps couples navigate cultural differences and build a marriage based on mutual respect.

Action Points:

- Have regular discussions about each partner's cultural expectations.

- Respect traditional values while ensuring both partners feel empowered in the marriage.

- Set boundaries with extended family to create a healthy balance between family involvement and personal privacy.

2. Financial Expectations and Responsibilities

In Igbo culture, financial provision is often seen as a marker of responsibility, with men traditionally taking on the role of primary providers. Non-Igbo women may come from cultures where financial responsibilities are shared more equally or financial independence is emphasized for both partners. Addressing these financial differences is essential to avoiding tension and ensuring a stable family structure.

Couples must have open and honest conversations about financial expectations, including how household expenses will be divided, how family obligations will be managed, and how long-term financial goals will be set. While financial pressures, especially around extended family support, may be a source of conflict, setting clear financial boundaries and working together to create a shared budget can help alleviate stress.

Action Points:

- Establish a shared financial plan that includes short-term and long-term goals.

- Discuss family obligations and set boundaries for financial contributions to extended family members.

- Practice financial transparency to build trust and avoid misunderstandings.

3. The Role of Elders and Ancestral Legacy

In Igbo culture, elders are revered as custodians of family traditions and values, often playing a role in important decisions, including marriage and conflict resolution. Ancestral legacy also significantly shapes family identity, with rituals, stories, and traditions passed down through generations. For non-Igbo women, navigating this influence may feel overwhelming, especially if they come from cultures where independence and privacy in marital matters are more emphasized.

However, learning to appreciate the wisdom and role of elders in Igbo culture can strengthen the couple's connection to family heritage. By involving elders in important family decisions and participating in rituals that honour ancestral legacy, couples can build a bridge between the past and the future. Non-Igbo women can embrace these traditions while also creating space for new customs that reflect both sides of the family's cultural heritage.

Action Points:

- Involve elders in significant family discussions to honour their roles and contributions.

- Balance traditional rituals and ancestral practices with modern family life to create new family traditions.

- Ensure that both partners feel respected in family matters by setting boundaries and maintaining open communication.

4. Raising Bicultural Children

Raising bicultural children is one of cross-cultural marriages' most rewarding yet challenging aspects. These children grow up navigating two distinct cultural identities, learning to balance the traditions, values, and expectations of both parents. For Igbo men, passing down cultural values such as respect for elders, family responsibility, and the Igbo language is a priority. At the same time, non-Igbo women may emphasize individualism, independence, and a different set of traditions.

Parents in cross-cultural marriages must work together to raise their children in an environment that celebrates both sides of their heritage. Encouraging bilingualism or multilingualism, blending cultural traditions, and helping children build a confident sense of identity are key strategies for ensuring that children feel proud of their unique background. This also helps children develop a global perspective and greater adaptability, which are invaluable in today's diverse world.

Action Points:

- Create an environment that supports bilingualism or multilingualism to ensure children remain connected to both cultures.

- Celebrate both cultures through family traditions and holidays to help children appreciate their heritage.

- Provide emotional support for children navigating identity challenges by encouraging them to embrace both sides of their cultural background.

5. Addressing Misconceptions in Cross-Cultural Marriages

Misconceptions about Igbo men—whether related to traditional gender roles, financial expectations, or emotional expression—can sometimes create tension in cross-cultural marriages. Non-Igbo women may have preconceived notions about how their Igbo husbands will approach marriage, especially if they are unfamiliar with the intricacies of Igbo culture. On the other hand, Igbo men may face the challenge of adapting to more egalitarian or independent approaches to marriage.

Addressing these misconceptions early in the relationship is essential for building trust and understanding. By dispelling stereotypes and embracing each other's cultural values, couples can overcome the challenges of miscommunication and create a partnership that reflects mutual respect and shared goals.

Action Points:

- Encourage open dialogue to dispel misconceptions or stereotypes about Igbo men or cross-cultural marriage.

- Be willing to adapt and compromise when cultural differences arise while respecting each other's traditions.

- Build a marriage based on shared values rather than preconceived notions about gender roles or cultural expectations.

6. Conflict Resolution in Cross-Cultural Marriages

Conflict is inevitable in cross-cultural marriages, particularly when navigating cultural differences. However, how couples resolve these conflicts can strengthen their relationship or lead to further tension. In Igbo culture, elders often play a role in conflict resolution, offering advice and mediating disputes to maintain family harmony. Non-Igbo women, who may be accustomed to handling conflicts privately, may initially find this practice unfamiliar.

Couples must establish a conflict resolution strategy that honours both partners' preferences. This may involve seeking advice from elders while also ensuring that the couple feels empowered to resolve issues independently when necessary. Effective conflict resolution requires patience, communication, and a willingness to understand each other's cultural approaches to resolving disagreements.

Action Points:

- Develop a conflict resolution strategy that includes both traditional and modern approaches.

- Involve elders when necessary while maintaining privacy and autonomy in the marriage.

- Practice patience and empathy, recognizing that cultural differences can influence conflict approaches.

Conclusion: Leveraging the Value of Cross-Cultural Marriages

Cross-cultural marriages between Igbo men and non-Igbo women offer incredible opportunities for growth and understanding. They create a unique family dynamic that honours both cultural backgrounds. By embracing each other's traditions, values, and perspectives, couples can build a marriage that reflects mutual respect, shared goals, and a deep sense of cultural pride.

However, it is essential to approach these relationships with caution and care. This report is provided for informational purposes only and should not be taken as professional counsel to enter into a relationship that may not be healthy or beneficial. Before making any decisions about marriage or family, conducting thorough research, consulting with family members, and seeking professional advice when needed is essential. Entering a relationship, particularly one that involves navigating two different cultures, requires a commitment to understanding, compromise, and personal growth.

We welcome feedback from readers on how this report can be improved for future publication. If you have any suggestions, comments, or experiences, we encourage you to provide feedback to help others navigate the complexities of cross-cultural marriages. Your input will allow us to refine the content, ensuring that future readers benefit from a well-rounded, insightful guide.

Request for Feedback

We invite you to share your thoughts on this report and provide suggestions for improvement. Your feedback is invaluable in helping us offer more comprehensive and relevant information to readers interested in cross-cultural marriages. Please reach out with your comments and let us know how this report has helped you and what topics or areas you'd like to explore further. Together, we can create a resource that continues to empower and guide individuals navigating cross-cultural relationships.

BIBLIOGRAPHY

Achebe, C. (2012). *There was a country: A personal history of Biafra.* Penguin Books.

Braun, V., & Clarke, V. (2006). Using thematic analysis in psychology. *Qualitative Research in Psychology, 3*(2), 77-101. https://doi.org/10.1191/1478088706qp063oa

Bourdieu, P. (1986). The forms of capital. In J. G. Richardson (Ed.), *Handbook of theory and research for the sociology of education* (pp. 241-258). Greenwood Press.

Chukwudi, O. (2021). The Igbo Apprenticeship System: A case study of entrepreneurship and wealth creation in Southeastern Nigeria. *Journal of African Business, 22*(1), 1-16. https://doi.org/10.1080/15228916.2020.1861572

Creswell, J. W., & Poth, C. N. (2018). *Qualitative inquiry and research design: Choosing among five approaches* (4th ed.). SAGE Publications.

Eke, P. (2023). Marrying an Igbo man: Perspectives from non-Igbo women. *Cross-Cultural Marriage Journal, 15*(2), 67-83.

Ezeh, G. (2021). Changing family structures in Igbo society: From extended to nuclear families. *Nigerian Journal of Sociological Studies, 24*(3), 45-60.

Falicov, C. J. (2014). *Latino families in therapy* (2nd ed.). Guilford Press.

Gaines, S. O., Jr., Ramkumar, N. A., Kumar, P. N., & Rios, D. I. (1997). Impact of cross-cultural and interracial romantic relationships on identity development. *Journal of Social and Personal Relationships,* *14*(3), 335-356. https://doi.org/10.1177/0265407597143003

Guest, G., Bunce, A., & Johnson, L. (2006). How many interviews are enough? An experiment with data saturation and variability. *Field Methods, 18*(1), 59-82. https://doi.org/10.1177/1525822X05279903

Ilogu, E. (1974). *Christianity and Ibo culture: A study of the interaction of Christianity and Ibo culture.* Brill.

Isichei, E. (1977). *A history of the Igbo people.* Macmillan.

Krippendorff, K. (2018). *Content analysis: An introduction to its methodology* (4th ed.). SAGE Publications.

Kvale, S., & Brinkmann, S. (2009). *Interviews: Learning the craft of qualitative research interviewing* (2nd ed.). SAGE Publications.

Mbah, E. (2022). Perceptions of Igbo men in cross-cultural marriages: A study of cultural integration. *International Journal of Marriage Studies, 9*(1), 102-119. https://doi.org/10.1080/22233754.2022.978326

Mok, T. A. (2020). Cross-cultural marriages in a globalized world. *Global Sociological Review, 5*(1), 24-39.

Morgan, D. L. (1997). *Focus groups as qualitative research* (2nd ed.). SAGE Publications.

Nnamani, C. (2022). Igbo marriages in a globalized world: Navigating cross-cultural unions. *Nigerian Journal of Cultural Studies, 18*(2), 56-70.

Njoku, O. (2020). The role of Umunna in Igbo marriages: Family, society, and tradition. *Nigerian Cultural Review, 12*(1), 55-72.

Nwoye, A. (2011). The praxis of indigenous social work in Africa: A case study of the Igbo of Nigeria. *International Social Work, 54*(5), 656-672. https://doi.org/10.1177/0020872810396363

Okafor, J., & Amaka, P. (2018). Gender roles in contemporary Igbo society: The shifting dynamics. *Journal of African Studies, 22*(4), 78-91.

Okeke-Ihejirika, P., & Salami, B. (2018). *Negotiating power and place: Transnationalism and gender in African-Canadian families.* University of Toronto Press.

Onyeozili, E. C., & Ebbe, O. N. I. (2012). Social control in precolonial Igbo society. *African Journal of Criminology and Justice Studies, 6*(1), 28-43.

Patton, M. Q. (2015). *Qualitative research & evaluation methods* (4th ed.). SAGE Publications.

Saldana, J. (2013). *The coding manual for qualitative researchers* (2nd ed.). SAGE Publications.

Smith, J. A., Flowers, P., & Larkin, M. (2009). *Interpretative phenomenological analysis: Theory, method and research.* SAGE Publications.

Ting-Toomey, S. (2010). Intercultural competence in cross-cultural relationships. *International Journal of Intercultural Relations, 34*(4), 236-247. https://doi.org/10.1016/j.ijintrel.2010.03.003

Tizard, B., & Phoenix, A. (2002). *Black, white or mixed race? Race and racism in the lives of young people of mixed parentage.* Routledge.

Uchendu, V. C. (2016). *The Igbo of Southeast Nigeria.* Holt, Rinehart, and Winston.

Umejesi, I. (2020). Igbo diaspora: Global influences and cultural practices. *The African Diaspora Review, 7*(3), 42-58.

ABOUT THE AUTHOR

DR. GODWIN UDE is a distinguished clinical counsellor, psychotherapist, author, conference speaker, personal development and Emotional intelligence (EI) consultant, and academic with an extensive psychology and positive psychiatry background. He holds a Bachelor of Pharmacy, a master's in counselling, and an MBA (master's in business administration). He also completed a Positive Psychology and Psychiatry certificate from the University of Sydney, Australia. Further enhancing his expertise, Dr. Ude earned a Professional Higher Education Certificate from Harvard University and a Doctor of Philosophy in Interdisciplinary Studies and Social Research from Oxford Graduate School. Dr. Ude heads a Community-University Engagement Research Project at the University of British Columbia, Canada. As the Executive Director of Kingdom Acts Foundation, Dr. Ude has successfully consulted and/or delivered projects for the Ministry of Agric and Agri-food, Canadian Heritage, Employment and Social Development Canada (ESDC), Vancouver Foundation, United Way British Columbia, Foundation for Black Communities, Surrey Cares Community Foundation and the Government of British Columbia. Dr. Ude has produced research reports focusing on Black Canadians for the Ministry of Canadian Heritage, the Canadian Women Foundation and the Vancouver Foundation.

With over fifteen years of experience, Dr. Ude has dedicated his career to working with diverse communities across Canada and the United States, specializing in clinical counselling and psychotherapy.

His expertise extends to public policy, where he has made significant contributions as a consultant and advocate for marginalized communities. Dr. Ude has represented these groups at the United Nations Permanent Forum in Geneva, Switzerland, advocating for policies that support their well-being and integration into society.

As a community leader, Dr. Ude is committed to helping individuals better understand themselves and develop essential soft skills for success in both personal and professional realms. His global experience and passionate advocacy for mental health and education make him a respected voice in psychology, public policy, social research, and community development.

www.ingramcontent.com/pod-product-compliance
Lightning Source LLC
Chambersburg PA
CBHW060836280326
41934CB00007B/801